THE ORIGINS OF
STRATEGIC BOMBING

The Origins of
Strategic Bombing

A Study of the Development of
British Air Strategic Thought
and Practice upto 1918.

NEVILLE JONES

WILLIAM KIMBER · LONDON

First published in 1973 by
WILLIAM KIMBER & CO. LIMITED
Godolphin House, 22a Queen Anne's Gate,
London, SW1H 9AE.

© Neville Jones, 1973
ISBN 07183 0093 9

Typeset by
Specialised Offset Services Ltd, Liverpool,
and printed in Great Britain by
Robert MacLehose & Co. Ltd, Glasgow.

Contents

List of Illustrations

To the Memory of
the Second Earl of Halsbury
who made an outstanding contribution
to strategic air thought during the
First World War.

Abbreviations used in the Text

A A   Anti-aircraft
B E F   British Expeditionary Force
C A S   Chief of the Air Staff
C I D   Committee of Imperial Defence
C I G S   Chief of the Imperial General Staff
C T D   Controller of the Technical Department (Air Ministry)
D A S   Director of Air Services (Admiralty)
D C A S   Deputy Chief of the Air Staff
D/F   Direction Finding
D F O   Director of Flying Operations (Air Ministry)
G H Q   General Headquarters
G O C   General Officer Commanding
I F   Independent Force
J W A C   Joint War Air Committee
O C   Officer Commanding
R F C   Royal Flying Corps
R N A S   Royal Naval Air Service
R U S I   Royal United Service Institution
W O   War Office
W/T   Wireless Telegraphy

Acknowledgements

The author wishes to thank the Controller of Her Majesty's Stationery Office for permission to quote from Crown — copyright records held in the Public Records Office and to use photographic illustrations of material from the same source.

He also wishes to thank the following for permission to quote from printed copyright material: The Clarendon Press, Oxford for the extracts from *The War in the Air* by Walter Raleigh and H.A. Jones; William Collins and Co., Ltd., for the extracts from *Trenchard* by Andrew Boyle; Peter Davies Ltd., for the extracts from *Sagittarius Rising* by Cecil Lewis and *Sailor in the Air* by Vice-Admiral R.B. Davies; Faber and Faber Ltd., for the extract from *Behind the Smoke Screen* by Brigadier-General P.R.C. Groves; George G. Harrap and Co., for the extracts from *From Many Angles* by Major-General Sir Frederick Sykes; I P C Transport Press Ltd., for the extracts from *Flight, The Aeroplane* and *Flying*; Werner Laurie and Co., Ltd., for the extract from *Vision Ahead* by Air Commodore P. Huskinson.

He also wishes to thank the Earl of Halsbury for his kind help in answering many questions about his father and in making available his father's papers. He is grateful for permission to quote from these papers.

He also wishes to express his thanks to Wing Commander T.E.W. Browne, G.J. Holdcroft and J.A. Stedman who provided him with much valuable information relating to their operational experiences with the bomber squadrons at Nancy (1917-18).

He also wishes to thank Chaz Bowyer, G. Stuart Leslie and R.C.B. Ashworth for their help in providing the photographic illustrations.

Special thanks are due to my wife who typed a difficult manuscript and to my colleague, D.R. Zelley, who drew the map and the bomb-sighting diagram.

Introduction

Strategic bombing may be defined as the direct attack against the most important elements of an enemy's war-making capacity, for example, his industries, communications, and the morale of his civilian population, as opposed to the units and equipment of his armed forces. The object of such bombing, which is the product of an age in which the distinction between soldier and civilian has disappeared, is to undermine the enemy's war effort.[1]

Strategic bombing was first used by the British air services in the First World War; but it was not employed on a large scale until the Second World War, during which it was developed by the Royal Air Force into a weapon of great destructive power. Yet, for much of the first half of the Second World War, the bombing, which was carried out at long range from bases in England, was largely ineffective.[2] From the outset serious operational difficulties were encountered. During the early months of the war the day bombers suffered so severely from the action of German fighters that bombing in daylight was soon abandoned. By the spring of 1940 the offensive was carried out almost entirely at night.[3] Under the cover of darkness the bombers were able to evade the enemy fighters, but this immunity from attack was bought at a high price. The bomber crews, with nothing save the most primitive methods of navigation to aid them, experienced the greatest difficulty in finding their way in the dark and could seldom locate and hit their targets. As a result the greater part of the bombing effort was wasted.

It was not until 1942, with the introduction of new navigational and bombing aids and improved operational techniques, that the damage inflicted on the German war machine bore some relation to the expenditure of resources on the bomber force. From then on, the strategic offensive became an increasingly important factor in the final defeat of Germany.

When, at the end of the war, the suspected failure of the early offensive was confirmed by evidence collected in Germany, explanations were sought to account for this. Without doubt, the reason most generally accepted in the Royal Air Force was that the experience and knowledge of strategic warfare provided by the First World War were so slight as to be of negligible value in preparing for the second war against Germany.

What had to be learnt, it was believed, could only have been learnt through the actual operations of war. In consequence, mistakes were inevitable in the early stages.[4]

Broadly speaking, it is impossible to quarrel with this view. It is certainly true that strategic bombing was practised on only a small scale during the First World War. But what of the implication that almost nothing was discovered about the nature of strategic warfare? Equally certainly, this is not true. From 1916 onwards, and especially during the last year of the war, much work, involving practical experiments, operational research and staff planning, was undertaken in this field and a considerable body of knowledge assembled. In particular, the main problems concerned with strategic bombing were identified, and in most cases action had been taken to investigate them. Twenty years later, however, on the eve of the Second World War, the fact that these problems even existed had long since been forgotten. For example, in 1918, the difficulties of navigation, especially at night, on the long-distance flights often involved in strategic bombing were fully appreciated, and the need for bombs that were designed for use against specific types of targets was recognized. Yet in 1939 no advance had been made in the techniques of navigation or in the design of bombs.

These facts point to the situation which prevailed during the First World War, namely, that strategic bombing was reckoned of small importance, air power being used almost exclusively as an auxiliary of military and naval operations. They indicate, too, that the work of the small minority who advocated direct attacks against the war centres of Germany was neither understood nor appreciated at the time and was forgotten as soon as the war was over.

During the whole of the First World War the greater part of Britain's air strength was committed to the tactical support of the British Army on the Western Front. Such strategic operations as were undertaken before the formation of the Royal Air Force in 1918, were carried out by the Royal Naval Air Service. Indeed, it was a matter of deliberate policy that the Royal Flying Corps was developed purely as an auxiliary of the land forces. In the first phase of the war the squadrons attached to the British Expeditionary Force were used exclusively for reconnaissance, but with the emergence of trench warfare their duties were extended to include, among other things, photography, artillery spotting and patrolling. The majority of this work was of a non-offensive nature; the truly offensive elements of air co-operation – air fighting and bombing – were developed slowly and unsystematically.

Soon after the outbreak of war, the developing land battle in France became the focal point of action, and the same precedence which was given to the provision of men and material for the army units on the Western Front was accorded to the supply of personnel and aircraft for the squadrons supporting them. As the scale of the fighting in the west increased, more and more effort was directed to the tactical air war. In consequence, there were never sufficient resources to create a force of aircraft specifically designed for strategic bombing – a type of air warfare which was constantly adding to the number of its influential supporters.

As was to be expected, the military air leaders, who held that the sole raison d'être for the existence of the Flying Corps was army support, resisted every attempt to form a strategic bomber force, being convinced that strategic bombing was a luxury so long as the air requirements of the Army were not met in full. It was not until the last few months of the war — for political and not military reasons — that a systematic bombardment of war centres in Germany was undertaken; and even then the strength of the force assembled to carry out the offensive never attained more than a handful of squadrons.

The role of the military squadrons was firmly established by the beginning of the war and the officer who exerted the greatest influence in this direction was General Sir David Henderson, the first Director-General of Military Aeronautics. Henderson, a reconnaissance expert and the author of a well-known book on the subject, was quick to appreciate the potential of the aeroplane as an instrument of reconnaissance. After taking his pilot's certificate in 1911, he did much to encourage interest in military aviation; and when the Royal Flying Corps was created in 1912 he greatly influenced the development of the Military Wing as a reconnaissance force. His concept of military aeroplanes as slow unarmed machines moving leisurely above the battlefield in search of intelligence for the army staffs was one which impressed itself upon the military squadrons. When war broke out he took command of the Flying Corps in France and laid the foundations of the extended air support which was provided for the British Expeditionary Force.

After less than a year in this command, Sir David Henderson felt himself compelled to return to the War Office as head of the aeronautical department. He was succeeded in France by the most remarkable of the leaders of the Flying Corps, General Hugh M. Trenchard, who remained in command of the R.F.C. in-the-Field until the formation of the Royal Air Force in 1918 and was the first Chief of the Air Staff in the newly created service. Like his predecessor, General Trenchard regarded the Flying Corps as an integral part of the Army and opposed the use of aircraft other than in direct co-operation with the land forces.

Holding as they did the two key posts in the ever-growing air service, Henderson and Trenchard were able to resist the pressures exerted by those who believed that air attacks directed against German war industry would make an effective contribution to the winning of the war. Whenever the question of this type of bombing was raised, they insisted that the necessary air support must first be provided for the Army before men and aircraft were devoted to strategic bombing — a condition which virtually ruled out a strategic offensive, for the estimates of army requirements were always in excess of what British resources could provide. Naturally, this policy was supported by Sir Douglas Haig, the Commander-in-Chief of the British Armies in France, and so won Government approval.

An understanding of British air policy must be sought in the concepts which guided General Trenchard in his command of the R.F.C. in France. As has been stated, he conceived of air power purely in terms of the support it could provide for the Army, believing that every available aircraft should be committed to the battle on the Western Front. This was a corollary of the prevailing military view that the war could only be won on this front and that any diversion of strength to other theatres merely weakened the power of attack in the vital sector. It was never doubted that the German line could be breached if assaults on a sufficiently heavy scale were launched. The great advantages which rapid-firing weapons and wire entrenchments conferred upon the defence were consistently underestimated.

Beginning with the attack at Neuve Chapelle in March 1915, a series of onslaughts was made, each of them intended to drive through to open country beyond the enemy lines; but the expected break-through was not achieved. Gains in territory were insignificant, while the cost in lives became progressively higher.

In spite of the early failures, Sir Douglas Haig remained confident that he could achieve his aims by these battering-ram tactics, and in planning for attacks on an ever increasing scale he

B

received the dedicated support of General Trenchard who matched the offensive on the ground with an offensive in the air, maintained whenever possible and at whatever the cost. It was this facet of Trenchard's policy more than any other which had a decisive effect on Britain's air strategy. It involved carrying the air war to the enemy at all times and cost the Flying Corps dearly in casualties; for on every possible occasion British aircraft flew over or behind the enemy lines where they naturally operated at a great disadvantage.[5]

Owing to the heavy losses which he sustained, Trenchard was compelled to make incessant demands for replacements of men and aircraft; and this, combined with the need for an ever increasing number of squadrons to keep pace with the growing strength of the British Expeditionary Force, led him to use his considerable influence with Haig to prevent the use of aircraft on strategic bombing. The most serious threat to his supply of new aircraft was, in his view, the formation by the Admiralty, in 1916, of a strategic bomber force based in Lorraine. Trenchard took up the matter with Haig and was therefore able to register his protests at the highest level. As a result of Haig's intervention the naval force was disbanded.[6]

Trenchard maintained his opposition to strategic bombing until the end of the war. Even when, in the autumn of 1917, the Government decreed the formation of a bomber force to attack targets in Germany in retaliation for German aeroplane raids on London, he made no secret of his disagreement with this decision. It was therefore one of the major ironies of the war when, in the summer of 1918, this force was expanded to form the Independent Force – to carry out a systematic bombardment of German industrial centres – Trenchard was appointed to command it.

Trenchard's command in France had a profound influence on the development of British military aviation. Owing to the high priority he assigned to certain duties, the Army concentrated almost wholly on the production of reconnaissance and fighting aircraft. Air bombing was regarded as a secondary duty and almost no aircraft were designed specifically for this work. Consequently, the problems relating to bombing tactics and the development of bombs and bombsights received little attention. Often, however, tactical bombing was carried out on a considerable scale, especially during the great battles of the war. But because of the prevailing ignorance of air bombing, losses were generally high in relation to the damage inflicted upon the enemy. For the most part, these operations were carried out by reconnaissance aircraft which were employed for bombing only when the need arose. In addition to the unsuitability of many of the aircraft, the pilots who flew them received no training in this highly specialized work.

The Navy, on the other hand, attached the highest importance to all types of bombing and devoted much effort to the development of both day and night bombers and to the study of bombing techniques. For the same reason, special training was provided for naval personnel who were destined for bomber squadrons. In the early months of the war naval air units carried out the first raids against targets in Germany, and by the end of 1915 plans were in hand for a systematic offensive against German industrial centres. The leaders of the Royal Naval Air Service were convinced that strategic bombing had a valuable part to play in the air war and made great efforts to provide suitable aircraft and equipment for this work. But their endeavours were constantly frustrated by the opposition of the leaders of the Flying Corps. It was not until 1917 when the Government, under pressure from Parliament and the public, resolved to create a strategic bomber force that the results of the naval work were manifested. The last year of the war, therefore, showed remarkable advances in the techniques and equipment concerned with strategic bombing.

The Navy had long recognized that accurate navigation was essential to the success of strategic bombing, which was frequently directed against targets at long range. Before the end of 1917 the Admiralty had made provision for the training of pilots and observers, of both air services, in the techniques of navigation on long-distance flights.[7] Early in 1918 the scheme was extended, and special schools were opened to provide a combined course in navigation and bombing.[8] It was also appreciated that successful navigation was dependent to an important degree upon the accuracy with which an aircraft course could be set. Up to 1918, aircraft compasses were generally unreliable, but in that year the long and detailed study carried out by the Admiralty Compass Observatory culminated in the invention of the aperiodic compass, which represented the greatest advance in design since the first truly air compass was produced in 1911.[9]

Naval methods of navigation required that crews should, while in the air, be able to plot bearings and courses and keep a constant check on the speed and direction of the wind. This was opposed to the Flying Corps method of relying mainly on forecast winds for both navigation and bombing. Mindful of the difficult conditions under which crews worked during flights, the Navy had given much thought to the design of instruments which would enable navigational problems to be solved quickly and with acceptable accuracy in the air. By the summer of 1918 several of these instruments were being manufactured in quantity, and distribution to the squadrons had begun.[10]

By 1918, too, navigation by direction-finding (D/F) wireless telegraphy (W/T) had been improved and extended.[11] This method of position finding had first been used by the naval squadrons at Dunkirk as a navigational aid for aircraft operating against enemy bases in Belgium.[12] Experiments at the R.N.A.S. station at Cranwell had resulted in improved direction-finding techniques, and by the middle of the year arrangements were in hand to provide D/F facilities for the squadrons of the Independent Force that were to bomb targets in Germany direct from bases in East Anglia.[13]

Nor had the Navy neglected to develop the bombsight, the instrument upon whose efficiency the success of bombing raids finally depended. For much of the war the typical bombsight was a somewhat crude instrument of limited accuracy. It required the use of a stop watch for setting and could be used effectively only when the aircraft was flying up or down wind.[14] Then, late in 1917, the most significant bombsight of the war was first tested. It was the course-setting bombsight designed by a naval officer, Lieutenant-Commander H.E. Wimperis. This sight required no stop watch and allowed an aircraft to attack from any angle irrespective of the direction of the wind.[15]

Advances in the design of bomber aircraft during the last year of the war could hardly have been so impressive, for at least as early as the summer of 1916 the long-range bomber had, chiefly through the efforts of the Navy, been an effective weapon. The Sopwith day bombers of the naval wing at Luxeuil (1916–1917) had operated almost with impunity against targets in Germany and German occupied Lorraine. Later, the day squadrons of the bomber force at Nancy, operating with D.H.4's and D.H.9's, successfully attacked a wide range of targets in the same area, in spite of fierce German opposition.

The standard night bomber was the Handley Page 0-400 which operated with conspicuous success with the naval squadrons at Dunkirk and with the force at Nancy. However, a new important night bomber, which like the 0-400 was designed to naval specifications, made its appearance in 1918. It was the Handley Page V-1500, the first and last British four-engined aircraft to be produced before 1941. This aircraft was expected to have the range to fly to Berlin and back from a base in England, but the war ended before it went into squadron service.[16]

When the R.N.A.S. and R.F.C. were amalgamated to form the Royal Air Force the new service was nearer in character and outlook to the military than to the naval air service. This was so, not only because the R.F.C. was the larger service and therefore provided most of the senior officers for the R.A.F., but also because of the immense personal prestige enjoyed by Trenchard who held the post of Chief of the Air Staff almost continuously from 1918 to 1929. It was therefore to be expected that the account of the air war which began to take shape in the years immediately following the war derived largely from the tradition of the military service. So strong indeed was that tradition that Sir Walter Raleigh and H.A. Jones, the authors of the Official History, *The War in the Air*, which is still the most detailed and authoritative work on the subject, were profoundly influenced by it.

This influence is particularly marked in the first volume, by Sir Walter Raleigh, which contains a detailed account of the origins and development of military and naval aviation in Britain. Here, it is taken for granted that the Military Wing of the Flying Corps would become a reconnaissance unit of the proposed British Expeditionary Force, and in support of this assumption, the first military aeroplane squadrons are shown to be the direct descendants of the early balloon units which were used by the British Army for field reconnaissance. From this account it is not possible to discern the real reason why military aviation first began to receive serious attention in this country. This was because of widespread fears that the fleet of airships which was being built in Germany would be capable of delivering bombing attacks against Britain.

In response to these fears, the Government directed the War Office to investigate the possible danger from air attack and to consider the best means of defence against it. Strangely, the action taken by the Army was to create a force of reconnaissance aircraft, the whole of which accompanied the B.E.F. to France at the outbreak of war. Arrangements for the air defence of Britain were not even begun.

On the death of Sir Walter Raleigh, who completed only the first volume of the history, the work was continued by H.A. Jones, who, though more independent than his predecessor, still followed the lines of the established tradition. The narrative of events after the outbreak of war treats the complete subordination of the growing air service to the requirements of the Army almost as a pre-determined order of things. Thus, the extension of the tactical duties of the squadrons and the policy of the offensive are assumed to be part of that order. The consistent advocacy, by the

Air Department of the Admiralty, of a strategic bombing effort, and the equally consistent opposition of the military air leaders to the use of air strength for that purpose is hardly mentioned. Indeed, it is impossible to discern from the Official History the extent to which the Admiralty and the War Office were divided on this important question.

Perhaps the best example of how naval strategic policy and operations are virtually ignored in the history is provided by the story of No. 3 Naval Wing at Luxeuil. This wing was raised as a bomber force to carry out raids against Germany and German occupied territory, in conjunction with the French. It began to operate in the summer of 1916 and was disbanded in the spring of 1917, as a result of protests from the military air leaders. The operations of this wing are a landmark in the history of the British air services for they represent the first planned offensive aimed directly against the enemy's war centres. It is true that the operations were carried out on only a small scale — the result of constant army demands for naval aircraft — but this fact does not detract from their importance in the development of air warfare. Yet the Admiralty plans for the strategic offensive do not even find a place in the history, and the actual operations of the wing occupy a mere seven pages, two in Volume II and five in Volume VI.[17]

At the end of the passage in Volume VI the Official Historian acknowledges that the naval operations were far more successful than they were given credit for at the time; but quite unfairly he lays the blame for the disbandment of No. 3 Wing upon Sir Douglas Haig, who had written to the Air Board to complain that the naval force was being used on operations which were properly the concern of the Army.

But it is clear from the evidence that the opposition to the naval wing was initiated by Sir David Henderson, in London, and was taken up in France by General Trenchard. It is true that the letter which was decisive in settling the fate of the naval bombers was signed by Haig, but there is little doubt that it was written from a draft prepared by Trenchard. In any case, it is most unlikely that Haig, who a few months earlier had stated categorically that he had no objections to the naval operations, would have taken this action unless the question of the naval squadrons had been raised again by Trenchard.

Thus *The War in the Air* gives an incomplete account of the history of British military and naval aviation from its origins to the end of the First World War. And since the majority of subsequent works dealing with British air power during this period have relied heavily upon the Official History for their material, this version has become the most widely accepted one. Now, however, the official documents relating to the whole of this period are open to inspection and the inadequacies of this account may be corrected. This important source of information has therefore been made the basis of this study which seeks to shed light on that aspect of air power to which the Official Historians devoted so little attention, namely, the development of air strategic thought and practice.

Chapter 1

The Development of
Strategic Thought up to 1914

The essence of strategic bombing is the offensive, and the first interest in the flying machine as a potentially offensive weapon goes back at least to 1907. In that year the Hague Conference, an international gathering to explore the possibilities of arms reductions, met for the second time. One of the items before the Conference was a proposal to renew an article, which had expired since its ratification at the first meeting of the Conference in 1899, prohibiting the dropping of projectiles and explosives from flying machines.[1] The majority of the powers refused to renew the article, and the chief reason for this action was the belief that since flying machines engaged on military operations would certainly be fired upon they should not be deprived of the means of retaliation. Instead, it was agreed that the limitations already imposed upon land and sea forces, namely, that the bombardment of undefended places was forbidden, should apply equally to air machines.[2] The attitude adopted suggests that many of the nations were unwilling to forgo the possible advantages of using these machines in an offensive capacity.

In 1907, too, the idea of using the airship for long-range bombardment was first brought to the public notice. This was in *The War in the Air*, a story by H.G. Wells, in which the author pictured a devastating attack upon the city of New York by a fleet of airships. There is no doubt that the interest aroused by this story was enhanced by the probability that the Zeppelin type of airship, then being developed in Germany, would soon be capable of flying long distances.

Even at this early date the powerful continental countries were well ahead of Britain in the field of aeronautics, and the implications of this situation were not lost upon the military authorities in this country. In October 1908, the Committee of Imperial Defence nominated a sub-committee under Lord Esher to investigate 'the dangers to which we would be exposed on sea or on land by any developments in aerial navigation reasonably probable in the near future' and to decide in the light of the knowledge thus gained 'the naval and military advantages that we might expect to derive from the use of airships or aeroplanes'. The report of the sub-committee, issued in January 1909, contained a clear warning that it would be folly to underestimate the possible dangers from air attack in the foreseeable future. The following extract from the conclusions of the report sums up the committee's findings.

Although in the existing state of aerial navigation Great Britain is not exposed to any serious danger by land, it would be improvident and possibly dangerous to assume that the rapid developments which the art of aerostatics has recently made may not entail in the near future risks by land and sea.

Invasion of Great Britain in airships on a large scale may be dismissed as unlikely for many years to come.... It is conceivable, however, that these machines might be employed for conveying a small raiding force for such a purpose as inflicting a damaging blow to an arsenal or dockyard.

Furthermore, attacks upon warships and dockyards by dropping explosives and incendiary bombs onto them from dirigible balloons, though at present in an experimental stage, cannot be dismissed as an impossible operation of war, and it is doubtful whether our men-of-war and coast defences possess adequate means to ward them off. In view of the experiments which are being carried out on the continent, it appears desirable that experiments should also be undertaken in this country to ascertain how far accurate results can be obtained by dropping objects on to a target from various heights.

It seems certain also that even in their existing state of development, dirigible balloons might be employed in naval warfare to ascertain the movements of fleets and to give warning of attack. No means can at present be suggested for preventing this.

The evidence before the Committee tends to show that the full potentialities of the air-ships, and the dangers to which we might be exposed by their use, can only be ascertained definitely by building them ourselves. This was the original reason for constructing submarines, and in their case the policy has since been completely vindicated.[3]

The report of the Esher Committee appeared at the beginning of a year which was remarkable in the pre-war period for the formation of a body of opinion which recognized the growing offensive power of the air machine and the extreme vulnerability of Britain to air attack.

Among those who were influenced by these considerations Lord Montagu of Beaulieu was perhaps the first to translate the notion of vulnerability into terms of actual injury that might be inflicted upon Britain. On 21st April 1909, at a meeting of the National Defence Association, he described the probable effect of a raid on London by a fleet of airships. He conceived the attack as directed against what he called the 'nerve centres' of the capital, the Houses of Parliament, the Government offices, the General Post Office, and the telephone exchanges, among others, the destruction of which would paralyse the nation. He believed that airships would strike so swiftly, and with such devastating results, that the country's defences would be powerless to intervene effectively.[4]

Two convictions are implicit in Lord Montagu's speech. First, the combatants in a major war of the future would not hesitate to use air bombardment if they thought it would contribute to a decisive victory; and secondly, London, the heart of Britain and her Empire, was unique in importance and vulnerability as a target for air attack. It is worthy of note that when the substance of the first of these points was raised in a House of Commons debate on airships in war, on 2nd August 1909, doubts were expressed as to whether some nations would even scruple to terrorize civilians by air bombing in order to compel an enemy to sue for peace.[5]

Meanwhile, early in 1909, the Aerial League of the British Empire was founded 'to secure and maintain for the Empire the same supremacy in the Air as it now enjoys on the Sea'.[6] Owing to the support it received from many influential persons, including Lord Roberts, the Marquis of Salisbury, H.G. Wells, Lord Esher and Lord Montagu of Beaulieu, the League was able to secure the nomination to its council of representatives from several government departments, including the Admiralty, the War Office and the Board of Trade.[7]

Though the League described itself as a 'strictly non-party organisation', with the implication that its objectives were non-political, it could hardly have forwarded its cause without criticizing the Government's lack of policy concerning military aviation. Indeed, the Government's apparent indifference to the development of military flying in other countries was causing uneasiness in many quarters, and this was increased when, on 25th July 1909, the Frenchman Louis Blériot flew the English Channel in an aeroplane of his own design. This flight offered irrefutable proof that Britain could no longer depend on her island position for protection against attack. It also served as a reminder that the aeroplane as well as the airship might be developed for offensive duties.

After Blériot's memorable achievement, it was more frequently asked what Britain was doing to match the progress being made in military aeronautics by the continental powers. At a meeting of the Royal United Service Institution, on 8th December 1909, Lord Roberts stated that the progress being made by Germany and France served to remind us of our own backwardness.

A writer in *Flight*, using Lord Roberts's statement as a starting point, was more forthright in his criticism of the Government's inaction.

There is unfortunately no indication at all as yet that the claims of the aeroplane in its military application have been adequately considered, or that the authorities have taken any steps at all to commence the systematic training of any considerable body of men in readiness for the inevitable developments of the near future.[8]

On the occasion of Lord Roberts's comment at the Royal United Service Institution, Major B.F.S. Baden-Powell had read a paper entitled 'How Airships are likely to Affect War'. The speaker said he believed that the danger from air attack was great and that it was necessary to prepare for defence on land against this type of warfare.[9]

In 1910, the mounting criticism of the Government's inaction was led by the Aerial League of the British Empire. The Admiralty view that the presence on the League's council of the representatives of government departments was 'the best way to ensure it being kept straight and not developing into an agitating body',[10] underestimated the tenacity of the League in pursuing its objectives. Without reference to the council, the executive committee launched a campaign to raise funds and enlist more support for the League's activities. The pamphlet which outlined the objects of the campaign criticized the Government for Britain's weakness in military aviation, and, as the following extracts show, emphasized the threat to Britain contained in Germany's air preparations.

The German Government had at its disposal at the end of 1909 a fleet of over 20 air vessels capable in favourable weather of fulfilling the scouting duties that are becoming more than ever necessary to military and naval strategy; also of transporting and discharging explosive material sufficient

completely to dislocate or totally destroy what Lord
Montagu of Beaulieu has aptly termed the 'nerve centres' of
our intricate systems of commerce and communication,
which are the life blood of our National and Imperial
existence.

Such a fleet (and it will shortly be tripled or quadrupled)
may be expected, in time of war, to do incalculable damage
to our docks, harbours, our reserves of ammunition and other
stores, our wireless stations and other centres of our complex
naval and military organisations.

Germany is building a great air fleet which can in no sense
be called 'defensive' nor perhaps of any great commercial
value; she is training officers and men at the rate of 2,000 per
annum and has already 10,000 men in her Aeronautical
Corps. She is building this air fleet because she recognises
that to be supreme in the air is of the most vital importance.
Air Power, in the near future, is likely to minimise the
supremacy which sea-power has hitherto conferred upon a
nation which possesses it.

Compared with the extraordinary energy and prescience
with which all nations are throwing themselves into the
development of aeroplanes and dirigible balloons, backed by
boundless public enthusiasm and state encouragement, the
backward position of this country, and the extraordinary
apathy of its people are deplorable to a degree.[11]

Suspicions of German ambitions were further increased when
the International Conference on Aerial Navigation opened in Paris
in May 1910. At the request of the French Government, Britain
had agreed to send a delegation, in the belief that discussions
would be confined to such topics as registration of airships,
customs regulations and rules of the road. When, however, the
German representatives raised issues of strategic importance,
strong objections were raised in this country, and these are
reflected in the following extracts from a memorandum submitted

by the General Staff to the Committee of Imperial Defence.

The General Staff learned, therefore, with some surprise, that, at the instance of Herr Kriege, the chief of the German Delegates, and with the support apparently of the French representatives, far-reaching proposals were being submitted to the Conference which had for their object the adoption of a declaration that the navigation of the air above foreign countries should be free in principle, and that foreign airships should not be treated less favourably than those of nationals. The insistence with which these proposals were being pressed by Germany could only lead to the conclusion that some ulterior object was in view, and in the opinion of the General Staff this object may be found in the desire of the German Government to have no restrictions as to the free movement of airships over the territories of the smaller States of Northern Europe, and as to their right to land in these territories for purposes of rest, repair, refitment, and the purchase of oil and other supplied or stores. The advantage to Germany of such an arrangement during a period of strained relations with Great Britain is obvious. Being comparatively weak in cruisers she may, it is thought, at such a time rely to a great extent upon her airships for a close reconnaissance of our coasts and harbours, and any restrictions as to passage over Holland and Belgium, or power to land at will in those countries would necessarily prove a source of embarrassment to her. This, however, is more a Naval than a Military question.

The second of the German contentions also appeared to the General Staff to be objectionable from a military point of view. To admit the principle that foreign airships were not to be treated less favourably than national ones was tantamount to saying that foreign airships were to have the same privileges of passage over, say, the Thames or Portsmouth defences as our own Naval and Military airships.

Such proposals, the memorandum stated, were unacceptable; at the very least, the flight of foreign airships over areas vital to our defence should be prohibited.

In expressing their objection to the proposals put forward by Germany, the General Staff were at pains to emphasize their awareness that the mere rejection of these proposals would not halt the development of aviation in other countries or make Britain any safer from attack. If the science of aeronautics advanced sufficiently to enable airships 'to move with reasonable certainty and to drop explosives with reasonable accuracy on war vessels, docks, magazines, and factories of warlike stores' it would be up to us to devise means of protecting our vital centres. In effect, this would mean 'acquiring and maintaining, if not air command, at least air equality by developing guns and other appliances capable of destroying those airships, if in time of war they threaten our sea warships or approach our shores'.[1][2]

It will be noted that the views of those who believed that the air machine would be developed as a weapon of war have much in common. The main points of agreement may be summarized under three headings. First, the flying machine was capable of being used as an instrument of bombardment, and effective defence against air attack would be difficult to achieve. Secondly, Britain was especially vulnerable to attack since many of her most important civil and military centres were situated in that part of the country nearest to the continent. Thirdly, Britain must acquire her own flying machines in order to discover by experiment the tactics most likely to be used by an enemy, and from the knowledge gained to work out an appropriate system of defence.

If, therefore, the Government came to accept these arguments, and in doing so, admitted the need for a force of military and naval flying machines, it would be reasonable to assume that the principal aims of the Government in establishing an air service would be as follows: first, to provide a force of flying machines so that experiments might be carried out to discover the most suitable tactics for the use of such machines in war. Secondly, to discover with what accuracy and effect bombs could be dropped from the air on to targets on the ground. Thirdly, to construct a defence system against aerial attack. It will therefore be appropriate at this point to follow the steps towards the creation of a British air service, and to see how far that service was designed to meet the needs of the country as visualized by a considerable body of informed opinion.

Broadly speaking, the action which was required fell under one of two headings. First, it was necessary to increase our meagre knowledge concerning the construction of flying machines by a systematic study of the science of aeronautics, and to support this work by experiments in the laboratory and in the air. Secondly, there was the need to determine the part that airships and aeroplanes might be expected to play in a future war, and to make plans for their use by our own armed forces.

Government action on the first of these was taken soon after the Esher Committee reported its findings. A number of scientists, engineers, and military and naval officers with experience in aeronautics were invited to form a committee to investigate the problems concerning the design of flying machines. The committee, designated the Advisory Committee for Aeronautics, had as its president Lord Rayleigh, chairman of the National Physical Laboratory, and among its members were seven Fellows of the Royal Society. It carried out its work in close co-operation with the National Physical Laboratory, which organized a department specially equipped to perform experiments called for by the committee.[13]

The difficulties of tackling the problems under the second heading were formidable indeed. Few high ranking officers of either service were convinced that flying machines could be made to serve a useful purpose in war, and those who were so convinced could not agree among themselves whether precedence should be given to the development of lighter-than-air or heavier-than-air craft. A common view was that we should follow closely the progress of military aeronautics on the continent and postpone any action until much more information was available.

Certainly the Esher Committee's report created an awareness, both at the Admiralty and the War Office, of the considerable developments in military flying in other countries, especially in Germany and France. In 1909 the War Office began to compile reports dealing with military aviation in a wide range of foreign countries. The reports were produced annually for official circulation and cover the years 1909 to 1913.

The first report, dated 14th November 1909, shows that in Germany the possibility of using airships in an offensive capacity was already being explored, and experiments had been carried out to discover the vulnerability of dirigibles to gun-fire from the ground. The opinion of General Rohne, a German artillery expert, was that airships would prove the best defence against airships, but that effective anti-airship guns could be produced. The report makes clear that the idea of an airship fleet found much support among the German people. The early flights of the Zeppelins were followed by articles 'advocating the invasion of England in airships'. Also 'picture-cards representing the destruction of British cruisers by bombs from German dirigibles found a ready sale'. The military authorities in Germany were sceptical of such visionary ideas, and believed that strategic reconnaissance was at that time the limit of the airship's usefulness.[14]

The War Office reports both of 1909 and 1910 refer to bomb-dropping trials from airships carried out in Germany. The opinion expressed in the 1909 report was that so far as was known nothing of value had been achieved. In the report of 1910 it was stated that the dropping of explosives had taken place at the Cologne manoeuvres but that the results had been kept secret.[15]

The extent to which the development of military aviation on the continent posed a threat to this country was one of the factors considered by a standing committee, set up in July 1909 by the Committee of Imperial Defence, to advise the Government on the defence of ports in Great Britain.[16] It was however the Admiralty which took the initiative in regard to air defence. In January 1910 an Admiralty conference, attended by the heads of the interested naval departments, reviewed the whole question of the air defence of such naval installations as magazines and dockyards, and forwarded its recommendations to the War Office, on whom rested the responsibility for the defence of naval centres against air attack.[17]

Up to the formation of the Flying Corps in 1912, the armed services made little headway in the design and production of machines to meet their own requirements. Early in 1909 the not unsuccessful aeroplane experiments of S.F. Cody and Lieutenant J.W. Dunne, on behalf of the Army, were terminated because it was judged that too little progress had been made to warrant a further allocation of funds.[18] A few months after this decision was taken Blériot flew across the English Channel. In the same year, work was begun on the construction of the first naval rigid airship, popularly called the 'Mayfly', which in 1911 broke her back even before she had flown. After this setback the Admiralty decided that work on the construction of naval airships should be discontinued, and the special aeronautical section, under Captain Murray F. Sueter, was disbanded and its officers returned to general service.[19]

Finally, in 1911, it was decided that the time had come to fulfil the need for an organized military air service. The first step was the creation of the Air Battalion of the Royal Engineers, in April 1911, to supersede the Balloon School. The task of the new unit was to create 'a body of expert airmen', and in accordance with the War Office directive, a Headquarters and two companies, No. 1 (Airship) and No. 2 (Aeroplane) were established.[20] From the beginning, it was realized that the Air Battalion was too narrowly based, for its sole function was to perform reconnaissance duties for the army in the field; and during the year of its existence plans were discussed and drawn up for the formation of an air service to meet the needs of both the Navy and the Army.

Meanwhile, on a smaller scale, the Navy was renewing its interest in aviation. In 1911, four naval officers were given permission to take a flying course at Eastchurch.[2][1]

In November 1911, the Committee of Imperial Defence set up a Sub-Committee on Aerial Navigation and directed it to examine the whole problem of military aviation. With the minimum of delay, the sub-committee reported that a British aviation service, to be called the Flying Corps, should be formed, and that it should consist of a Naval Wing, a Military Wing, and a Central Flying School for the training of pilots of both services. Having made these broad recommendations, the committee delegated to a Technical Sub-Committee 'the task of elaborating all the details necessary to give immediate effect to the policy proposed.'[2][2]

The Chairman of the Technical Sub-Committee was Colonel J.E.B. Seely, Secretary of State for War; the Army was represented by two Brigadier-Generals, G.K. Scott-Moncrieff and D. Henderson, while the two naval representatives were a Commander and a Lieutenant. It will be seen that the Army possessed a greater weight of authority on the sub-committee than the Navy, yet even this fact does not fully explain why the committee's report was so completely orientated to military thinking. The document, which was produced under the names of all the committee members, was in fact compiled in private by four army officers, of whom only one, Brigadier-General Henderson, was a member of the committee.

This report, dated 17th February 1912, repays careful study because it reveals the lines on which British air thought was to be directed until the end of the First World War. It is, however, a curious document, for it wholly ignores the possibility of an air attack upon this country; an eventuality which had frequently preoccupied the Government since the appearance of the Esher Committee's report. In view of the findings of the Esher Committee and the weight of much informed opinion, it would be reasonable to expect the report of the Technical Sub-Committee to deal with air defence and to recommend experiments, in bomb-dropping for instance, to discover the nature of the damage that might be inflicted by enemy machines. In fact, neither of these received attention.

The report acknowledged the disparity between the military air preparations of other nations and our own, and emphasized that the necessity for an efficient aeronautical service in this country was no less urgent than in the case of other great naval and military powers. The necessity mentioned here did not relate to defence, or even to attack in retaliation for hostile action, but concerned the provision of the army with an effective reconnaissance force.

The efficiency of the aeroplane for purposes of military reconnaissance [the report stated] has been proved both in foreign manoeuvres and in actual warfare in Tripoli, and the sub-committee have no hesitation in recording their opinion that aeroplanes have now become an important adjunct to the equipment of an army in the field.

The sub-committee were much less certain about the functions of naval aircraft.

The strategical and tactical use of the aeroplane as an adjunct to the operations of a fleet [the report ran] cannot yet be forecasted with equal certainty, as the question depends largely upon the solution of the technical difficulties in rising from and alighting on a ship and in rising from and alighting on the water.

At any rate the sub-committee had no hesitation in stating that naval aircraft would have an important part to play in reconnaissance over the sea.

Clearly, the primary role of both naval and military aircraft was expected to be reconnaissance. There seemed to be little awareness of the fact that quite different types of aircraft would be required for different duties, as the following passage from the report shows.

While it is admitted that the needs of the Navy and Army differ, and that each requires technical development peculiar to sea and land warfare respectively, the foundation of the requirements of each service is identical, viz. an adequate number of efficient flying men. Hence, though each service requires an establishment suitable to its own special needs, the aerial branch of one service should be regarded as a reserve to the aerial branch of the other. Thus in a purely naval war the whole of the Flying Corps should be available to the Navy, and in purely land war the whole corps should be available to the Army.

On one point the report was absolutely clear. The military aircraft was first and foremost to be used as an auxiliary in land operations. There was no mention of its development as an active deferce against attacking airships, nor, strange to relate in a nation unlikely to submit passively to attack, any hint of its use as a retaliatory weapon against an aggressor. The functions that it was expected to fulfil in war were stated precisely, in order of priority. There were: (a) Reconnaissance (b) Prevention of the enemy's reconnaissance (c) Inter-communication (d) Observation of artillery fire (e) Infliction of damage on the enemy. It should be noted . ¹t (e) refers to the enemy army in the field and not to objectives outside the battle area.

Somewhat surprisingly, the recommendations of the Technical Sub-Committee were quickly approved by the Committee of Imperial Defence, and the Royal Flying Corps came into being in April 1912. It was intended that both wings of the new corps should work in the closest co-operation. Both naval and military pilots were to receive their training at the Central Flying School and from there were to be posted to the naval air station at Eastchurch or to one of the military squadrons to receive the appropriate specialist training in naval or military aviation. In the same way, the Aircraft Factory was intended to provide a service for both wings. In fact, from the first the Naval Wing went its own way. Naval pilots received their training *ab initio* at Eastchurch, and the Admiralty preferred to place contracts for experimental work and for the construction of aircraft with private firms rather than to make use of the Aircraft Factory. Even before the outbreak of war, the term Royal Flying Corps, Naval Wing, had been dropped and the title Royal Naval Air Service had taken its place.

At the end of 1912 new evidence of Germany's increasing efforts in the air was received. This was contained in a report submitted to the Admiralty by the British Naval and Military Attachés in Berlin.[23] The report pointed out that the German Government paid subsidies to firms engaged in the construction of airships, and by so doing, was able to insist that airships owned by private firms were maintained at a required standard of efficiency. This meant that at the outbreak of a war 'the naval and military authorities will thus have at their disposal not only the Government aircraft, but also a number of dirigible airships belonging to private firms fully manned and equipped and ready for instant service'. It was estimated that at the time of writing there were available a total of about twenty airships of which seven or eight were Zeppelins. Such a formidable fleet, it was believed, constituted a threat to Britain, for a number of the airships 'would be capable of sailing from Germany to Sheerness, Woolwich and any other desired point in England and return without the necessity of an intermediate descent to earth. Though none of these dirigibles are as yet capable of maintaining an average speed of 60 m.p.h., only very unfavourable winds could in most cases prevent the passage of the North Sea being carried out at rates less than 30 to 40 m.p.h.'.

Significant, too, for Britain was the reaction of the German public concerning the airship fleet.

For some time past [the report stated] the German nation has felt with pride and much patriotic satisfaction that in its airships it possesses an asset in wartime of no inconsiderable value. Particularly it is thought that in a war with England the unrivalled German dirigible might play an important role. It is indeed difficult not to believe that this notion of an aerial fleet, which might reduce or neutralise the superiority of the British Navy is responsible to a large degree for the bounding enthusiasm of the German people over their dirigible airships.

War with Britain was, it seemed, a constant theme in Germany, and the report cited a recent lecture given by a German naval captain at Kiel. This officer made repeated reference to a war with England, and stated that airships, by carrying the war into Britain itself, would not only cause serious material damage but would also strike at the morale of the people.

During the period up to the outbreak of war there emerged a marked contrast between the policies and activities of the two wings. As was to be expected, the Military Wing concentrated wholly on the formation of a force of reconnaissance aircraft. The best type of aeroplane for work with the Army was considered to be one which was slow and stable — characteristics which had obvious advantages in peace-time, but which proved to be disastrous in war. There is no evidence to show that any attempt was made to organize an air defence system. Certainly no progress was made in adapting guns for use against aircraft, nor was consideration given to the use of armed aeroplanes against hostile aircraft. There was, it is true, an experimental unit under Major H. Musgrave,[24] an able and imaginative officer, and a programme was laid down for experimental work; but the majority of the specified experiments were intended to improve the tactics of co-operation with the field forces.

There was, however, no place for the slow, unarmed aircraft in the plans of the Naval Wing. The naval aeroplane was conceived of as a weapon of offensive power even when used in defence. From the beginning, the Navy carried out trials with aero-engines of far greater power than the 100 horse-power maximum which had been imposed upon engines produced by the Aircraft Factory.[25] The machine-guns and bombs which naval aircraft were intended to carry could only be lifted by machines equipped with high-powered engines. The Admiralty took seriously the threat of the German airship, and envisaged attacks being made, mainly by night, on naval dockyards and installations. Experiments were carried out with special high-angle guns for use against airships, and consideration was even given to the possibility of mounting a gun in the basket of a kite balloon which, on the approach of raiders, would be flown over the objective to be defended.[26] Nevertheless it was believed that armed aeroplanes would provide the best defence against airships, and during 1913 trials were made with aeroplanes fitted with a maxim gun.

Although this work was to have far-reaching effects on naval air policy in the future, it had little or no influence on Britain's defence strategy at that time; for home defence was the responsibility of the War Office which jealously guarded its authority in this sphere.[27] It was not until after the outbreak of war, when the whole of the Military Wing had accompanied the British Expeditionary Force to France, leaving Britain without defence against air attack, that the Admiralty assumed responsibility for home defence.[28]

But the most striking contrast between the two air services is revealed in their approach to air navigation and bomb-dropping. While the Military Wing was building a force of aircraft quite unsuited to any offensive function, the Naval Wing visualized aeroplanes flying over considerable distances to bomb enemy naval craft, dockyards and shore installations.[29] It was already appreciated that an aircraft would have to be navigated, in much the same way as a ship, to reach its objective, and that on arrival at the target it must be able to aim its bombs accurately from various heights. And since accurate bomb-dropping depended largely upon the solution of basic navigational problems, the greater the degree of skill in navigation, the better the chances of successful

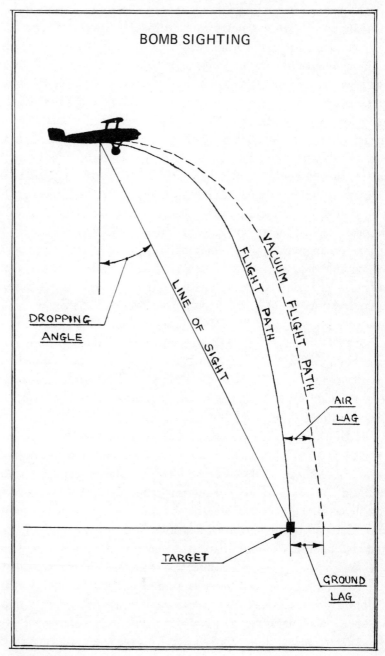

(Figure 1)

bombing. The fundamental requirement of air navigation is the determination of the speed and direction of the wind affecting the aircraft at the height it is flying. This information, together with the speed of the aircraft relative to the air, which is given by the airspeed indicator, will enable the navigator to calculate the course which the aircraft must set in order to make good a given direction over the ground (i.e. the track), the speed of the aircraft relative to the ground (i.e. the ground speed), and the time required to fly along that track to reach an objective whose distance from base is known. The problem involved in bomb-dropping is to determine the point at which a bomb must be released in order to strike a given target on the ground. This was done by means of an instrument which related information concerning the height and ground speed of the aircraft and the ballistic characteristics of the bomb in order to indicate the correct angle between the aircraft and the target at the point of release. This was known as the dropping angle and all bombsights, whatever their means of construction or method of operation, were designed to indicate this angle.[30] (See Figure 1, p. 42).

The interest of naval personnel in air navigation dates to the early days of flying in this country. The first published manual of air navigation was written by a naval officer,[31] and the first purely aircraft compass was designed by an officer of that service.[32] When the Royal Flying Corps came into being, the members of the Naval Wing applied their knowledge of sea navigation to overcome the difficulties of navigating in the air. For instance, in 1913, a Lieutenant Sitwell produced a circular slide rule for calculating the number of degrees that an aircraft must fly into wind in order to make good a given track.[33] This was one of the earliest of the many instruments designed by naval personnel for enabling navigational problems to be solved quickly, and with acceptable accuracy, under the difficult conditions experienced in the air.

On the other hand, air navigation in the Military Wing meant no more than the ability to map-read in the limited area of operations in the field. Yet even this modest requirement did not seem to have counted for much, for no provision was made for an adequate supply of maps. Many accounts are given by officers of the R.F.C. of the use, both before and during the war, of the map in Bradshaw's Railway Guide to navigate along railway lines.[34] Air Commodore P. Huskinson tells of a cross-country flight he made by this method early in 1916. 'I was solely dependent, as was then the established practice, on the map contained in Bradshaw's Railway Guide. However, by a close study of this, known throughout the Flying Corps as the Pilot's Friend, and by repeated low dives on stations along the line, I was able, in spite of the maddening fact that most of the stations appeared to bear no name but OXO, to grope my way home in reasonably good time.'[35]

Air Commodore Huskinson would not however have experienced these difficulties if early members of the R.F.C. had had their way. For in February 1914 the Officer Commanding No. 2 Squadron suggested to Headquarters, R.F.C. that the names of railway stations should be painted on the roofs of station buildings to assist navigation; and two months later the Officer Commanding No. 6 Squadron added the suggestion that the names of towns should be painted on gasometers.[36] Though these ideas were duly forwarded to the War Office, nothing apparently came of them.

It is difficult to trace in exact detail the bomb-dropping experiments carried out in the pre-war period by the two wings of the R.F.C.; but it is certain that at end of the Corps' first year of existence the Naval Wing had made considerable progress in trials with bombs, bomb-release gear and bombsights.[37] The first annual report on the Royal Flying Corps, dated 7th June 1913, described the naval experiments, but made no mention of any work in relation to bomb-dropping or aerial defence in the Military Wing. Concerning home defence, the report issued this warning:

The urgency of obtaining as soon as possible guns suitable for attacking aircraft has recently been forced into prominence by the realization that it is possible for German airships of the Zeppelin type to cross the North Sea and pass over this country, thus exposing ships, magazines and other vulnerable points to danger from attack with explosives.[38]

If this statement, which contained nothing which had not been known for some time, was intended to stir the Military Wing into action, it failed to achieve its purpose.

Thereafter, the Naval Wing increased the scope of its bombing and gunnery experiments. Extensive trials were made with various machine-guns fitted to aircraft, and considerable success was attained when a kite, which when towed by a ship reached a speed of over 60 m.p.h., was fired on from the air. Experiments with bombs of various shapes and weights were made to discover which types of bombs fell with the greatest accuracy. By the spring of 1914 a design of bomb-dropping gear which had proved successful during trials at Eastchurch was produced by the Ordnance Factory at Woolwich Arsenal.[39]

The first type of bombsight used by the Naval wing was held in the hand. It was levelled by means of a well-damped pendulum and the correct dropping angle (previously determined by inspecting tables for height and ground speed) was indicated on a scale of angles.[40] Towards the end of 1913, tests were carried out on a type of sight which was fixed to the aircraft. This was the Travers bombsight, the invention of Lieutenant Travers of the Royal Navy. The principal feature of this sight was that it measured the speed of the aircraft relative to the target by means of a clockwork motor. The motor controlled the speed of a moving foresight which had to be kept in line with the backsight and the target. The backsight was set against a scale which indicated the height of the aircraft. The movement of the foresight was translated automatically to a contact arm which completed an electrical circuit and dropped the bomb. Thus, the greater the speed of the aircraft, the faster the foresight had to be moved, and in consequence, the earlier the circuit was completed and the bomb released. Like many bombsights which incorporated mechanical devices for measuring ground speed, the Travers sight was difficult to operate owing to the pitching motion of the aircraft, and was too cumbersome to be fixed conveniently on the side of the fuselage. The report on the Travers sight recognized that it was an advanced instrument for its day, but concluded that it was not practical for use in the air.[41]

Little seems to have been accomplished in the Military Wing in regard to bomb-dropping and air defence. In August 1913 kites were used as targets for ground to air firing to discover with what accuracy moving targets in the air could be hit. It is doubtful whether anything worthwhile came out of the trials, for in April 1914 the War Office were pressing for a continuation of this work. After considerable delays, arrangements were made for further experiments to be made, at the Larkhill ranges, in July 1914. The kites were flown between three hundred and five hundred feet, at about 30 m.p.h., but since enemy aircraft were unlikely to offer themselves as targets at that speed and height the results of the firing were of negligible value.[42]

The question of attacking airships from the air was first raised by the War Office in October 1913. The Officer Commanding the Military Wing was asked whether it would be possible to devise some kind of bomb which could be suspended by a wire about three hundred feet below an aeroplane and fired electrically as a means of destroying airships. Before the end of the year experiments were started in what was called 'sweeping for airships with explosives trailing from aeroplanes', but by April 1914 work was at a stay because of the lack of a suitable aircraft. Nothing more was done before the outbreak of war.[43]

In the second annual report on the Royal Flying Corps, the only reference to bomb-dropping in the Military Wing was in a list of miscellaneous experiments.[44] Just how much was done may be judged from a report submitted by the Officer Commanding No. 3 Squadron in May 1913. The report contained the results of experiments carried out by four aircraft at heights varying from two hundred to eighteen hundred feet, during which '2 lb. bags of flour in tissue paper bags' were used 'to see if bombs dropped from above would hit the target aimed at'.[45] At the same time experiments were being carried out in the airship 'Beta'. A plumb-line was suspended from the airship, the object being to determine when the airship was vertically over the mark to be aimed at. The bomb was then released and the distance in yards that it undershot the target was recorded. It is difficult to see how a plumb-line could have been used to give an accurate vertical sight line when the airship was moving in a forward direction; and this may explain why 'the preliminary trials did not prove of value'. Further trials were made, and as a result, it was decided to replace the plumb-line by a sight which was being constructed in May 1913.[46] There is however no evidence to show whether the sight was ever completed or the trials resumed.

Almost certainly no systematic tests with bombsights were carried out by the Military Wing before the outbreak of war. At the end of 1913 Major Musgrave, the officer in charge of experiments, had tested in the air a ground speed indicator which it was thought could be adapted as a bombsight. The instrument was similar in principle to the Travers sight, and like the latter was too heavy and bulky to be used easily in the air. In May 1914 Major Musgrave wrote to the inventor and pointed out that although the instrument might with considerable modification prove of value as a sighting apparatus, a simpler type of sight would probably be more effective.[47]

Soon afterwards another design of sight was forwarded to the Military Wing for testing. It was the Coursin-Chauviere sight which its manufacturers stated was the type of sight used by the first and second prize winners at the last Michelin bomb-dropping competition. It is most unlikely that the sight was ever given a trial in the air, for a year and a half later the War Office, in response to enquiries from the manufacturers, were trying to locate the instrument which had been supplied to them in July 1914.[48] Finally, in the last few weeks of peace, the War Office made arrangements for the despatch of a bombsight manufactured by a German firm in Hamburg, but the war intervened before the order could be fulfilled.[49]

Thus, when war came in August 1914, the differences in policy and approach which had separated the two services since the early days of the Royal Flying Corps had become even more pronounced. Under the vigorous and resourceful leadership of Winston Churchill, the Navy had devoted its efforts to the creation of an essentially offensive air service. Attack was the keynote of naval policy, whether in planning to defend important centres in this country against hostile airships or to strike with aircraft at enemy naval targets. On the other hand, the aeroplanes of the Military Wing were intended to serve as the eyes of the Army. There were, it is true, vague ideas that aircraft might have to fight in the air to preserve their ability to fly over territory occupied by enemy forces, and to prevent enemy aeroplanes from carrying out similar flights over British positions. But in August 1914 not even the first steps had been taken to make possible such offensive action. Similarly, it was visualized that aeroplanes might be used to drop missiles on to enemy positions in the field, but such operations, it was believed, would be entirely subordinate to reconnaissance missions. The peacetime training of the Military Wing was therefore almost entirely devoted to the perfecting of techniques to provide the field commanders with the quickest and most accurate information concerning the movements and dispositions of enemy forces.

Yet even a glance at the work of the Military Wing from 1912 to 1914 will show that no less important than the wing's efforts to improve its performance as a reconnaissance force was the need to convince the army commanders themselves that there was a real need for air reconnaissance. 'Tell Sykes he is wasting his time; flying can never be of any use to the Army,' was the comment of Sir Douglas Haig in 1911 when he learned of that officer's interest in flying. Without doubt, Sir Frederick Sykes was correct in attributing Haig's hostility to flying to the fact that he was 'intensely jealous of anything which might seem to impair the paramountcy of his favourite arm, the cavalry'.

Again, Sykes records that in July 1914 Haig told his officers, 'I hope none of you gentlemen is so foolish as to think that aeroplanes will be able to be usefully employed for reconnaissance purposes in war. There is only one way for a commander to get information by reconnaissance, and that is by the use of cavalry.'[50] It may well be that the feverish endeavours of the military air commanders to overcome the General Staff's prejudice against flying was partly responsible for depressing any imaginative approach to the use of aircraft in war, and led to a concentration of attention upon the narrow objective of proving the flying service to be a legitimate extension of the cavalry arm.

D

Chapter 2

The Beginning of Air Bombing and the First Strategic Operations

In June 1914, the aeroplane squadrons of the Military Wing had, on the orders of Lieutenant-Colonel F.H. Sykes, commander of the Wing, gathered at Netheravon. By this time there were four squadrons destined for service with the B.E.F.: No. 2 Squadron and No. 4 Squadron equipped with B.E.2 aircraft, No. 3 Squadron with Blériots and Henri Farmans, and No. 5 Squadron with Henri Farmans, Avros and B.E.8's. During the remaining weeks of peace, intensive flying practice and ground training were carried out, and the arrangements for despatching the Wing to France were perfected.[1] When war came, plans were at once put into operation to send every aircraft that was fit for active service to the continent.

Sir David Henderson, Director-General of Military Aeronautics, assumed command of the force, and as soon as the last aeroplane had taken off safely, he crossed to Calais with his staff.[2] The transfer of the force across the Channel was achieved without incident. One difficulty alone is mentioned by Sir Frederick Sykes in his autobiography. While on its way to the rendezvous at Dover, No. 4 Squadron was delayed by the rumour of a Zeppelin raid on Woolwich. The squadron was at once despatched to Eastchurch where it remained until the alarm proved to be false.[3] It does not seem to have occurred to Sykes, nor indeed to anyone else in the Corps, that the Germans, who had airships ready for immediate service, might have taken advantage of the confusion which followed Britain's entry into the war to make harassing raids in the area of London and the Thames estuary.

Only a remnant of the Corps remained in England after the five squadrons had departed on 13th August. Though more than a hundred aircraft were left, only about twenty were fit to be used even for instructional purposes.[4] The officers who remained at home were given the unenviable task of creating new units out of almost nothing. One of these officers, Major H.M. Trenchard, though dismayed at being denied a part in the action, worked with great energy to assemble the aircraft, material and men out of which, first, reserves, which the B.E.F. squadrons totally lacked, and later, new squadrons were created.[5] More serious, Sir David Henderson took with him to France all the most experienced staff officers. The Aeronautical Department at the War Office was left in the hands of a few comparatively inexperienced men of junior rank at the very time when a first-rate staff, led by a man of recognized authority, was required to plan for the rapid expansion of the air service.

At this time, too, the tactics to be used in the various areas of air activity should have been evolved from the experience of war, and a programme of experimentation initiated to evaluate these tactics and to estimate the kinds of new equipment that would be required for the future. In fact none of this planning was carried out, and it is to this early period of the war that the future difficulties of the military air service may be traced.

Soon after the arrival of the squadrons in the battle area a general withdrawal of British forces was ordered. Much has been written about the value of air reconnaissance during the retreat from Mons. One thing alone is certain; it did not influence the conduct or outcome of that phase of the campaign which ended with the battle of the Marne. Nonetheless, the Flying Corps had achieved what it had set out to do, namely, to be at the front when the action started, to maintain aircraft in the air at every available opportunity, and to keep General Headquarters informed of intelligence gained from air observation: in short, to prove its viability and efficiency as a reconnaissance force under conditions of war. When however the war of mobility ended with the so-called 'race to the sea', the task for which the Flying Corps had prepared itself was largely at an end. But in the new conditions of war, in which two powerful armies were entrenched behind seemingly impregnable fortifications, the Flying Corps undertook a wide range of new duties, and in doing so, sought to demonstrate not merely its utility but also its indispensability to the British Army. With such single-minded purpose did the commanders of the Corps apply themselves to these new duties that they did not consider the possibility of using air power other than in the tactical role.

The effort required by the Flying Corps to adapt itself to its new duties, which included artillery spotting, photographic reconnaissance and bombing, was immense. One of the chief difficulties was the lack of aeroplanes, either in service or in the course of production, which were capable of lifting the extra weight in cameras, wireless equipment, bombs and so forth, without serious loss of performance. The main type of aircraft which had been planned before the war, and which began to be produced in large numbers in 1915, was the slow, unmanoeuvrable reconnaissance aircraft such as the B.E.2. In the early part of the war, the extreme vulnerability of this type of machine, weighed down by a variety of equipment, had hardly been recognized, for neither side possessed an aircraft of sufficient offensive power to force down another aircraft. Occasional air skirmishes with rifles and revolvers are recorded, but these encounters were mere tokens of an aggressive spirit. The complete lack of any systematic investigation, even after the outbreak of war, into the qualities required of aircraft which were to be assigned to specific duties, led to an unconscious acceptance of the 'all-purpose' aeroplane, invariably a machine intended for reconnaissance, which was called upon to perform whatever duties the occasion demanded, and which performed none of them efficiently.

An early example of this trend of thought is shown in a memorandum written at Headquarters, R.F.C. in October 1914, and addressed to Major Musgrave at the W/T Unit in France.

> Several instances [it stated] have occurred lately in which
> targets suitable for attack have been passed over without any
> action being taken. In future all aeroplanes carrying out
> reconnaissances will carry bombs, and whenever suitable
> targets ... present themselves, they should be attacked by
> dropping bombs.[6]

Major Musgrave disagreed emphatically with the instruction. In
his reply, he stated that aircraft on reconnaissance missions should
not be required to carry out bombing attacks as well. He pointed out
that quite different tactics were required for the two types of
operations. Bombing aircraft should carry as many bombs as
possible but no more fuel than was required to get to the target and
back with safety, and should steer direct for their objectives.
Reconnaissance aircraft, on the other hand, must always carry a
passenger to record observations and should carry a full load of fuel
to enable the aircraft to cover the maximum area during its time in
the air. These observations led Major Musgrave to describe what he
considered to be the most important characteristics of the bombing
machine. It should be fast, with a good rate of climb, must be able to
carry a worthwhile load of bombs, and should be so designed that
the pilot was afforded a clear view in front during the approach to
the target.[7]

More than a year after this correspondence C.G. Grey, the
editor of The Aeroplane, who never lacked reliable information on
service matters, criticized the British practice of using the
all-purpose aircraft. He noted that during the second half of 1915

> the various belligerent countries at last began to devote
> different types of aeroplanes to definite particular purposes,
> instead of using one unfortunate maid-of-all-work type for
> scouting, bombing, spotting, and fighting as occasion arose,
> and sending the poor thing up equipped equally inadequately
> for all the different jobs at once.

A serviceman with whom Grey had spoken had likened to a Christmas tree the 'machine loaded with a pilot and passenger, as much fuel as it will carry, machine-guns and ammunition, and then expecting it to carry "wireless", and a heavy camera, with a couple of dozen plates, and bombs as well'. Grey thought that the Christmas tree aeroplane was 'precisely the thing to avoid. Like everything which leads to diffusion of energy, it is bound to be inefficient. If aircraft are to be used to the best advantage they must be used for certain specific purposes, and no others'.[8]

The development of the Flying Corps in the early months of the war has been described in some detail because the later opposition to strategic bombing within the Corps may be traced to certain influences, and two in particular, which began to be felt during this period. First, the efforts of the Flying Corps to create for itself a permanent niche in the structure of the Army led to a concentration of attention on the requirements of the land forces, to the exclusion of a wider consideration of the use of air power. Secondly, the increasing reliance on the general purpose aircraft, and the failure to plan for the future development of aircraft designed for specific functions, resulted in losses which over a period diluted the skill and experience of the flying personnel. For instance, bombing raids carried out at any distance behind the German lines incurred losses quite out of proportion to the damage inflicted on the enemy. The air commanders therefore became increasingly reluctant to authorize bombing operations which involved more than a short flight over enemy-held territory. Long-distance bombing was therefore only rarely practised, and as pressure on the Corps to provide more direct army support continually increased, it ceased to be an important function of the service.

The alarm which had caused No. 4 Squadron to be sent to Eastchurch at the outbreak of war did not herald the beginning of a Zeppelin offensive against this country. Perhaps the false report of an attack on Woolwich sprang from the certainty in many minds that the Germans would not long delay their air assaults against England. It is indeed surprising that after creating, at great effort and cost, an airship force capable of bombing at long range the Germans should not have made plans for its use in a strategic role during the land offensive against France. The truth is that there was no place for an air campaign in the general war plan of the German High Command. During the few weeks the war was expected to last every effort was to be directed to the defeat of the French Army. Zeppelins were not used for strategic action until it was clear that the war would not be over quickly, and even then they were used merely for sporadic raiding. There was at no time any indication that the airship raids on Britain were planned to coincide with operations undertaken by German military or naval forces in other areas.

During the years before the war the German Army showed more interest in air power than the Navy, and was largely responsible for the creation of the airship fleet. On the outbreak of war, the Army possessed six Zeppelins, and shortly afterwards, three Zeppelins owned by civilian firms were equipped for war service and handed over to the military authorities. The nine army Zeppelins, together with the single Zeppelin of the German Navy, did not constitute a force as powerful as the Germans, some years before, had predicted they would possess, but it was nevertheless, numerically strong enough to have opened a campaign against Britain.

The Germany Army, however, was convinced of the value of airships in support of land operations, and it was in this role that they were first used – with disastrous results. During the first month of the war, three Zeppelins were lost on their first flights over the battle area, and the German airship force was reduced in strength by almost one third.[9] Then followed a reorganization in which the naval airship force was increased in strength and definite bases were established for both airship forces to begin operations against Britain. By the beginning of 1915, the naval airships were based on the north German coast, while the sheds in Belgium were allocated to the Army.[10]

It was fortunate that the Germans wasted their early opportunities. A series of raids on Britain at the time when the B.E.F. was in retreat would have been a shock to morale in this country. If such an attack had been made, the War Office would have been hard pressed to explain the lack of defence preparations. In the event, the War Office was relieved of the necessity of making any difficult explanations both then, and later when the Zeppelin raids began to pose a serious problem. The criticism for failing to prevent the raids was directed against the Admiralty, which, in response to Lord Kitchener's request, had assumed responsibility for home defence early in September 1914.

The first war task of the Admiralty was to organize air patrols along the east coast. When that was done air cover was provided for the passage of the B.E.F. across the Channel.[11] As soon as the British forces were safely across the water, offensive action against the enemy was begun. The first step was to send the naval squadron, commanded by Wing Commander C.R. Samson, from Eastchurch to Ostend where it was to operate with a force of marines.[12] Immediately on arrival, towards the end of August, the naval aeroplanes began to make daily reconnaissance flights over the area between Bruges, Ghent and Ypres; but the defence of Ostend against the advancing Germans was soon realized to be an impossible task for the lightly armed Marine Brigade, and on 30th August the marines and the aeroplane squadron were ordered to return at once to England. The force made its way back via Dunkirk and while held up at that port by the crash of a naval aeroplane it was instructed to remain there by an Admiralty telegram of 1st September. The Admiralty were resolved 'to deny the use of territory within a hundred miles of Dunkirk to German Zeppelins, and to attack by aeroplanes all airships found replenishing there'. In order to achieve this, the Admiralty proposed 'to place thirty or forty naval aeroplanes at Dunkirk or other convenient coast points' and 'to reinforce officer commanding aeroplanes with fifty to sixty armed motor-cars and two hundred to three hundred men'. The chief aim of these measures was to ensure 'the immunity of Portsmouth, Chatham, and London from dangerous aerial attack'.[13] With this message there began the long and successful naval operations from Dunkirk.

Wing Commander Samson, one of the most outstanding of the early naval fliers, is most often remembered for his daring exploits against the Germans with a small force of armoured cars, but he was also responsible for organizing the first air attacks against German territory. His small force of aeroplanes at Dunkirk was reinforced by aircraft from England, and plans were made to attack the airship sheds at Cologne and Düsseldorf by aircraft operating from Antwerp, which did not fall into German hands until 9th October. These were to be the first blows in the defence of Britain against the German airships. There were two raids, the first of which was carried out on 22nd September. Four aircraft were despatched, two to Cologne, and two to Düsseldorf, but only one pilot located his target, the shed at Düsseldorf, which he attacked from four hundred feet. It is probable that he hit the target, but some of his bombs failed to explode.[14] The second raid, which was more successful, was made on 8th October, the day that Antwerp was evacuated. The pilot of the aircraft which raided Düsseldorf attacked from six hundred feet and destroyed the shed and an airship inside it. The other pilot was unable to find the shed in the thick mist which shrouded Cologne so he dropped his bombs on the main railway station in the centre of the town.[15]

The fall of Antwerp was followed, on 15th October, by the German occupation of Zeebrugge and Ostend. The occupation of this coast by enemy forces created a serious situation for Britain, for the Germans were able to develop the harbours at Zeebrugge and Ostend as bases from which to attack allied shipping both at close and long range. The Admiralty reacted to this threat by building up a force of aeroplanes and seaplanes in the area of Dunkirk to keep up a constant attack against the German naval bases.[16] Undoubtedly this force did succeed in hindering enemy operations, but, as will be shown later, the bombing strength of these naval air units was so often dissipated, especially in operations in support of the Army, that the Germans suffered much less severely than they would have done if the force had been constituted as an independent formation.

The third naval raid against German territory was made on 21st November 1914 against the Zeppelin base at Friedrichshafen, on Lake Constance. The whole operation, which was planned to the last detail, was conducted in the greatest secrecy. The aircraft were transported by road at night to the aerodrome at Belfort from which the flight was made. Three Avro 504's took part in the raid and achieved complete surprise by approaching the target from over the lake. Considerable damage was done to a Zeppelin and the gas plant was destroyed. One aircraft was shot down by gunfire, its pilot being taken prisoner, but the other two returned safely to base, having completed a round flight of two hundred and fifty miles.[17]

The fourth naval raid was carried out by seaplanes on Christmas Day 1914, the object being to destroy the Zeppelin sheds at Cuxhaven. Three seaplane carriers, supported by a force of cruisers and destroyers, were engaged. Seven seaplanes were got away and though the Cuxhaven sheds could not be located in the poor visibility much useful information concerning the disposition of German naval forces was obtained, and some damage to shore installations was caused by bombing. Four seaplanes failed to return, but all the pilots were saved.[18]

It was no accident that all the early naval strategic operations were directed against the German Zeppelin force. When the Admiralty took over responsibility for home defence from the War Office on 3rd September, Winston Churchill, the First Lord, at once initiated an offensive policy to secure Britain from air attack. At a meeting of the War Council on 1st December 1914, Churchill stated that since 'it was impossible to provide effectively by means of passive defences for every vulnerable point liable to aircraft attack' the best policy 'was to attack the sheds and bases of the enemy's aircraft'.[19] Just how correct was that belief was

demonstrated by the remarkable success achieved by the four
naval raids of 1914. Clearly, Churchill intended to pursue an even
more aggressive air policy in 1915, when greater resources would be
available, and it is not improbable that if he had remained at the
Admiralty Britain might have possessed a strategic bomber force as
early as 1916. Unfortunately, Churchill was compelled to resign
his post in May 1915, and though the Naval Air Service never lost
the offensive spirit which he had fostered in it, henceforth the
Admiralty lacked a leader of his drive and authority to defend its
air policy against the strenuous opposition of the War Office.

During the first year of the war neither the R.N.A.S. nor the
R.F.C. possessed a force of aircraft capable of carrying out
sustained attacks, either at short or long range. Nevertheless, early
in 1915, both services were compelled by the exigencies of the war
to extend their bombing activities: the R.N.A.S. against the
Zeppelin sheds and German naval bases in Belgium, the R.F.C.
against targets in the area of the front. When the results of these
operations were analysed statistically in the summer of 1915, the
degree of success achieved – high for the naval squadrons and low
for the military squadrons – was seen to be related directly to the
effort which had been devoted to the problems of bombing.
Indeed, the work of the Navy to improve the equipment and
techniques of bombing was already beginning to produce results in
1915. The R.F.C., on the other hand, had focussed its attention
almost entirely on reconnaissance and as a result knew little of the
requirements of bombing.

As has been shown, the development of trench warfare forced
the Flying Corps to extend its range of air operations. Among the
most important of these new duties was that of bombing. By the
very nature of this type of warfare, large numbers of enemy troops
together with their impedimenta were to be found in the front line
and the area immediately behind it, so that there was no dearth of
targets for aircraft operating only a few miles from their bases.
Troops moving to and from the trench line, supplies of food,
equipment and ammunition being transported to the front, and

static targets such as billets, dumps and headquarters buildings all offered attractive targets for bombing. Though harassing raids of this kind were useful, bombing did not assume a role of great importance until the first of the allied offensives was launched in the spring of 1915. When an assault was made against the German line it was essential to prevent or delay the arrival of enemy reinforcements to the area under attack, and high priority was accorded to air bombing directed against the railway systems along which troops and supplies would be moved.

In anticipation of the effort that would be required of the military squadrons in the forthcoming offensives, Headquarters R.F.C. issued, in February 1915, a directive on bombing. The most significant feature of this document was that it stated what was desirable rather than what was possible, as the following extract shows.

Accuracy to within 50 yards is essential. If it cannot be obtained from heights of 5,000 to 6,000 feet, the target must be attacked at a low altitude — 500 feet.

Without adequate bombsights and bomb-release gear, accuracy of this order was impossible to attain from five thousand feet, and attacks at five hundred feet were likely to result in unacceptable high casualties. The directive showed an awareness of the need for special training for bombing operations, but none at all of the fact that specialized facilities and equipment and highly qualified instructors would be needed to carry out the training successfully. The solution to the problem of training offered in the directive was the one which, with unfortunate consequences for the standard of operational efficiency, was adopted in the Flying Corps until the end of 1917 — that of training on the squadrons. One flight from each squadron was to be detailed to carry out training in bomb-dropping and the various manoeuvres connected with bombing; but since only the most elementary equipment was available and no bombing tactics had been evolved by experimentation, it was futile to expect the squadrons to train themselves in a skill about which the service itself knew almost nothing. The directive contained a comprehensive list of the types of targets which should be attacked but offered no guidance as to the tactics to be employed.[20]

When the first of the British offensives opened at Neuve Chapelle, in March 1915, the weakness in air bombing was quickly exposed. The main objectives in all these early battles were the railways which the Germans would use to bring up reinforcements to the front. Though the individual squadrons themselves decided the tactics to be adopted, the most common practice was for aircraft to attack singly and at low level. The results obtained were on the whole poor, and it is not surprising that this was so. Indeed, the operations might have ended in complete failure if it had not been for the courage and determination of many pilots who, in the face of heavy fire from the ground, pressed home their attacks from suicidally low heights. For example, during the battle of Neuve Chapelle, Captain L.A. Strange of No. 6 Squadron dived so low to drop his bombs on Coutrai station that he almost collided with a line of telegraph poles. This pilot was fortunate to return safely to base, for his aeroplane was riddled with bullet holes.[21]

During the fighting in the Ypres salient, Courtrai was again an important objective. The Germans had apparently taken warning from earlier attacks, and when, on 26th April, Lieutenant W.B. Rhodes-Moorhouse of No. 2 Squadron bombed the station from three hundred feet he was met with heavy rifle and machine-gun fire. Though severely wounded, he was able to return to his own aerodrome, but died of his wounds on the following day. For this gallant exploit he was awarded the first Victoria Cross for work in the air.[22] It is not however inappropriate to remark that a type of operation which merits the highest award for gallantry is one which should not be repeated except in the most compelling circumstances. That Lieutenant Rhodes-Moorhouse adopted the only possible tactics to ensure a successful attack, as did many other pilots, is proof enough that the very limited success of these raids depended almost wholly on the courage and skill of the pilots and to a negligible degree on the equipment they used and the tactics in which they were trained.

Meanwhile, the Admiralty was faced with the dangerous situation which had resulted from the enemy occupation of Belgium. Before the end of 1914 German submarines had made their appearance at the Belgian bases, and early in the following year were operating widely in the waters around the British Isles. The military Zeppelin force, too, was able to take advantage of the favourable strategic situation. The airships could now be based in the Belgian sheds which were only a short flight from London.

The Admiralty responded to the crisis swiftly and predictably. The submarines and airships were to be attacked in their bases, and to this end a force of heavy bombers was planned. It was however impossible to begin operations on a sufficiently large scale for many months. The Navy possessed few aircraft capable of making bombing attacks, and even this small number was substantially reduced when, in February 1915, the unit at Dunkirk was sent to the Dardanelles – a campaign to which the Flying Corps was not required to make a contribution of aircraft.[23]

Nevertheless, naval raids, though of necessity light and sporadic, were carried out against the Belgian targets from early in 1915. Unlike the bombing operations of the Flying Corps, these were more successful and involved smaller losses, and were planned and executed with an awareness of the problems of tactics and equipment. It is instructive to compare a paper on bombing methods by Wing Commander Samson with the bombing directive issued by the Headquarters of the Flying Corps. Whereas the latter could offer no guidance on bombing tactics, Samson's paper described the various possible methods of attacking different targets.[24] Taken in conjunction with other reports compiled at that time, it provides certain evidence that the R.N.A.S. recognized the importance of keeping bombing tactics under constant scrutiny and of evaluating the effectiveness of each raid. The naval pilots, too, appreciated the importance of correct bombing techniques.

The report of an attack on submarines at Ostend, carried out by Squadron Commander S.D.A. Grey on 24th April 1915, may be used to illustrate this point.

> I located the submarines without any difficulty [wrote the pilot] and came down to 4,000 feet to attack them. I dropped a line of six bombs, starting just before my sights came on and finishing just after, to allow for any error in the estimated speed of the machine.[25]

Observations of this kind could not have been recorded by a Flying Corps pilot, for military aircraft had no bombsights and were for the most part fitted with bomb-release gear improvised on the squadrons, deficiencies which would have rendered an attack from four thousand feet an almost certain failure. Attacks such as those carried out by Captain Strange and Lieutenant Rhodes-Moorhouse were a melancholy pointer to the future; for because of unsuitable aeroplanes and poor equipment, military pilots were too often compelled to take unnecessary risks to have a chance of completing their missions successfully.

The urgency of hitting the German naval bases as hard and as quickly as possible induced the Navy, in the early months of 1915, to attempt too much with its slender resources. At first too many targets were attacked but it was soon realized that the weight of bombs which could be dropped on any one target was insufficient to cause more than the most minor inconvenience to the enemy. From April, therefore, the list of targets was reduced, and attention was concentrated on the nearer objectives.[26] Even so, the offensive capability of the aircraft operating from Dunkirk remained far below what was necessary to cause serious hindrance to the German naval operations. Nevertheless, the naval force persisted with the attacks and achieved a fair measure of success; but it was against the Zeppelins that a major victory was won.

By the beginning of May 1915 three military airships had arrived in Belgium, and by the end of that month one of them,

LZ38, had dropped the first bombs on London. Soon, however, the Zeppelins were to pay dearly for the advantage of operating at such short range from the British capital. In the early hours of 7th June, four naval aircraft left Dunkirk to attack the airship sheds at Evere and Berchem Ste. Agathe at the time that the three Zeppelins were on their way to England. One of the airships, LZ38 was forced by mechanical trouble to return to Evere. The other two, LZ37 and LZ39, lost their way in a thick mist and after unsuccessfully attempting to establish their positions altered course for base. When the naval attack on Evere began, LZ38 was already back in the shed. The bombs from the first aircraft damaged the shed; those from the second completely destroyed the airship. Meanwhile, Sub-Lieutenant R.A.J. Warneford was on his way to Berchem Ste. Agathe when he sighted LZ37. He took up the pursuit, and after outclimbing the airship, dropped his bombs along its whole length. The Zeppelin burst into flames and crashed. For this deed Warneford was awarded the Victoria Cross. Soon afterwards, the remaining Zeppelin was moved to the Russian front, and the Belgian sheds were definitely abandoned as permanent bases.[27]

Unfortunately, neither the British nor French military air services were achieving bombing results comparable to those of the Navy, a fact that is shown clearly in a memorandum prepared by the Headquarters of the Flying Corps in 1915. This contained an analysis of allied bombing results in the western theatre of operations from 1st March to 20th June 1915 and produced a depressing picture.

> The results obtained (except by the R.N.A.S.) [the report stated] are in no way commensurate with the efforts made, the risks incurred and the number of bombs dropped.

It was therefore apparent that 'as hitherto carried out by the French and British armies, aerial attack has not proved to be a serious operation of war'. If therefore the allied military bombing results should continue to be as 'disappointing' as in the period under review, 'it may be as well to eliminate bomb dropping altogether from their role, and to confine them to reconnaissance, observation for artillery and fighting in the air, in which they have proved their value and for which the Allies cannot have too many aeroplanes'.

Incorrect bombing methods and the choice of unsuitable objectives were the two reasons advanced to explain the poor results, but the vagueness of the terms used reveal how little the specific causes of failure were grasped. On the other hand, some of the factors which contributed to the achievement of the naval squadrons were understood.

The success obtained by the R.N.A.S., seems largely due to the fact that the efforts of the Wing at Dunkirk are concentrated almost solely on bomb dropping and that their pilots can be systematically trained for this one object.[28]

The evidence, both of success and failure, provided by the report pointed to the fact that bomb-dropping required specialized tactics and training, and from this it might have been inferred that specialized equipment, such as bombsights, bomb-release gear, and even specially designed aeroplanes, were essential.

This report was forwarded to British G.H.Q. where the main points were abstracted to form the basis of a letter sent to the three armies. The letter was based on an examination of the records of 483 bomb-dropping operations carried out between 1st April and 18th June 1915, in which 4,062 bombs were dropped by the R.F.C., the R.N.A.S. and the French air service. No attempt was made to show that the naval operations had achieved considerable success; all three services were stated to have attained small material results. However, the figures indicating percentage successes showed that of the attacks against Zeppelins in their sheds, mainly naval targets, 25% were successful, while only 2.1% of the operations against railway stations and junctions, mainly

Flying Corps targets, were successful. Indeed, the statement concerning railway bombing speaks for itself.

> Attempts to hinder the enemy's movements by bombing stations were made on 141 occasions during which 991 bombs were dropped. It appears that only three attempts were at all successful.

The purpose of these statistics was to show the need to adopt a new bombing policy. Henceforth, army commanders were to restrict bombing attacks by aeroplanes under their orders to a number of specified types of targets within the close reconnaissance area of the army. Whenever sustained bombing operations were required to disrupt the enemy's railway communications, these would be carried out under the authority of G.H.Q. as part of the overall allied operational plan.[29]

At any rate, neither the Flying Corps report nor the G.H.Q. directive could be criticized for attempting to minimize the extent of the bombing failure. Indeed, the directive restricting the scope of spasmodic bombing indicated that G.H.Q. were keenly aware of the import of the statistics. However, the report might be criticized for failing to offer constructive suggestions for repairing the deficiencies of the service. The attitude adopted was that since bombing had proved ineffective – for whatever reasons – it might be preferable to give up this type of operation and concentrate on such activities as reconnaissance and artillery spotting. It is true that the decision to persist with or to discontinue any kind of operation must to an important degree be influenced by the tactical feasibility of that operation. But here the question of feasibility was not at issue; for it was hardly possible to judge the feasibility of bombing when it was obvious that the reason for failing lay in the inadequacies of equipment, training and operational methods – all of which could have been improved, even with the resources then available.

The wholly negative approach reflected in the paper can only be comprehended against the background of the formation and development of the Flying Corps. From the outset, the Corps had eschewed any kind of offensive operation and had concentrated solely on reconnaissance work. And even in this limited area of activity the Corps was more suited to peace-time than to wartime operations. When therefore the bombing operations of the first half of 1915 ended in failure, there was a strong tendency among the Flying Corps staff, long conditioned to the idea of non-offensive army co-operation, to press for the reduction of bombing activity on the ground that the Corps did not possess sufficient resources even to fulfil its close support duties.

At this point there was still an influential supporter of air bombing at Flying Corps Headquarters. This was Colonel Sykes, who later became one of the leading advocates of strategic bombing. As Chief of the Air Staff during the last few months of the war, he did much to promote the idea of an allied strategic bomber force. If Sykes had assumed command of the R.F.C. in France, as he might well have done, he would certainly have developed the bomber element of the Corps. Equally certainly, he would have supported the naval strategic policy. Instead, Sykes was removed from the scene in France, and the post of General Officer Commanding was bestowed upon Trenchard, who immediately devoted himself to the task of organizing the Flying Corps wholly as an instrument of army support.

Trenchard's appointment as G.O.C. was a momentous one in the history of British military aviation. It not only influenced the course of events in the air during the First World War, but also gave direction to British air policy for the following twenty-five years. When the accounts of the air fighting in the 1914-18 War came to be written, Trenchard's fame was already secure. His successful struggle in the immediate post-war period to maintain the Air Force as an independent service had earned him the title of 'Father of the Royal Air Force' and he, almost alone of the generals who had served on the Western Front, was credited with having been successful in command. In restrospect, his appointment as G.O.C. in France was regarded as inevitable. In 1915 it was by no means inevitable, as a glance at his career and the circumstances of his appointment will show.

Trenchard entered the Army in 1893 and was commissioned in the Royal Scots Fusiliers.[30] The chief impression to be gained of him up to 1912 is that of an able and energic, though somewhat aggressive, officer who quarrelled with a succession of commanding officers. As an administrator he showed great flair but he could find only limited scope for his undoubted talents, for he did not pursue any course of military study to improve his prospects of promotion. In 1912, Trenchard was serving with the 2nd Battalion of his regiment in Londonderry. At 39, he was a major and had presumably reached the highest rank he was likely to attain. Then he was offered an unexpected opportunity of escaping from a life he found tedious and from a commanding officer with whom his relations were strained.[31] He secured his aviator's licence and by the end of August 1912 had arranged his transfer to the Flying Corps.[32] He was first posted to the Central Flying School at Upavon where, on account of his age and administrative experience, he became a member of the permanent staff as well as a pupil. Though he was an indifferent pilot, he was quickly recognized as an efficient administrator.[33]

On the outbreak of war Trenchard became commandant of the Military Wing in place of Sykes, who had gone to France as Chief of Staff to Sir David Henderson.[34] By this time Trenchard had formed a deep hatred of Sykes. Trenchard remained in England and for the next few months worked untiringly to lay the foundations for the expansion of the Corps. During this period he became known to Lord Kitchener, the Secretary of State for War, who was impressed by his energy and ability.[35]

In November 1914 Trenchard was given command of No. 1 Wing in France.[36] Shortly after his arrival in France, he discovered that Henderson had been appointed to command the 1st Division of the First Army Corps, under Sir Douglas Haig, and that Sykes was about to assume command of the R.F.C. 'The thought of serving under Sykes,' wrote his biographer, 'his junior in years and rank and someone he distrusted as a colleague and despised as a man, was intolerable.'[3][7]

Trenchard at once had a signal sent to the War Office requesting to be transferred to his old regiment and giving his reasons. The matter was apparently brought to the notice of Lord Kitchener who ordered both Henderson and Sykes to return to their former posts. In Sykes's case he gave inexperience as the reason for refusing to allow him to take command of the R.F.C.[38] However, a similar situation seemed likely to arise in the new year. The need for a senior officer to assume command of the aeronautical department at the War Office was already becoming apparent, and Henderson was the only officer with the necessary seniority and experience to fill the post. If Henderson should relinquish his post in France, the question of his successor would again cause trouble.

A further crisis was however averted, for in May 1915 Sykes was ordered by the War Office to proceed to the Dardanelles where he was to be responsible for planning for the employment of aircraft in the Gallipoli campaign.[39] There were no military aeroplanes in this theatre, only the R.N.A.S. contingent under Samson, and Sykes had to be invested with special naval ranks to enable him to carry out his duties.[40] In August 1915, when Henderson finally decided that his return to the War Office could no longer be postponed, Trenchard was appointed G.O.C. in France with the rank of Major-General.[41]

* * * *

High on the list of technical problems to be solved was that of bomb-aiming. It is true that the R.N.A.S. had, in the pre-war period, made considerable progress in the practice of aerial bombing, yet the problem of producing an effective bombsight still remained intractable at the outbreak of war. It was not that there were inherent difficulties in designing and making an instrument to indicate the correct dropping angle; the problems arose when the instrument was fitted to an aircraft. Apart from the difficulty of fixing the sight in such a position that it could easily be used by the pilot, there was the major problem of overcoming the effect on the sight caused by the slipstream and engine vibration. Many of the early sights incorporating a device for measuring ground speed were too cumbersome to be fitted in a suitable position, and were in any case most difficult to operate in the air.

After several unsuccessful experiments with various types of sights, the naval experimental flight turned to the production of a simple hand-held sight.[42] In its most elementary form the sight consisted of a board in which two pins or nails were positioned to indicate the correct dropping angle. When the sight was held level — this was indicated by means of a well-damped pendulum or spirit level — the correct instant of release was shown when the two pins were observed to be in line with the target. Such a fixed setting would however indicate the correct dropping angle only for a pre-determined height and ground speed. The next step was to devise a means by which the positions of the pins, and therefore the dropping angle, could be varied for different heights and ground speeds. This was achieved by mounting the two pins, that is, the foresight and backsight, on a lever pivoted at a point between them, so that the line of sight could be set at the correct dropping angle, which was determined by inspecting tables for height and ground speed. Such a device was known as the lever sight.[43]

Though simple in construction it was by no means easy to operate. During the approach to the target the pilot had, in addition to flying the aircraft 'straight and level', to hold the sight level, while at the same time keeping his eye in line with the foresight and backsight until the target crossed this line of sight. Nevertheless, the lever sight offered one immense advantage: it could be used in aircraft to which no fixed sight could be fitted owing to the poor view from the pilot's cockpit. Indeed, this type of sight was used with a reasonable degree of success by naval pilots, and as late as the spring of 1916 was still in use on naval flying training stations.

When the lever sight was sent to the R.F.C. for testing the reports were highly critical. Major Musgrave thought that it did not offer 'any advantages over existing sights'.[44] A Flying Corps pilot, Captain J.M.P. Reynolds, was more specific.

The spirit level is very slow in its working and insensitive to small measurements, and a very small error in sighting will make a big difference on the ground at 6,000 feet. The sights are too close together and difficult to align on the target.

His opinion was that the sight was unlikely to be of any use and was not worth testing on an aircraft.[45]

Meanwhile the Flying Corps were still trying to find a bombsight suitable for military aircraft, for unlike the R.N.A.S., they had no sight, adequate or otherwise, in service at the beginning of the war. At first, the War Office contemplated the construction of a sight designed as early as 1909, but finally rejected the idea because of difficulties in calibrating the instrument. Major Musgrave himself had designed a sight, and this, together with such sights as the Bristol, Blacker and Royal Aircraft Factory Bombsight Mk. 1, were tested unsuccessfully in the early part of the war. It is impossible to determine how assiduously the Flying Corps tried to find a suitable bombsight, but what is certain is that there was no co-ordination of the efforts of those who were working on the design of sights. Yet in spite of this, the first standard bombsight of the war was designed by an army officer, Lieutenant R.B. Bourdillon, who before the war had been a lecturer at the University of Oxford.

Towards the end of 1914 Lieutenant Bourdillon was an Intelligence Officer at a corps headquarters in France, and having much time on his hands he turned his attention to the design of a bombsight. When his work attracted attention, he applied to be seconded to the R.F.C. in order to devote more time to his invention, and was, in December 1914, transferred to the newly formed experimental flight at the Central Flying School. He soon discovered that the equipment and money made available to him were insufficient to enable him to make the somewhat complex sight he had designed in France. He therefore evolved a simpler sight whose principal feature was a time scale which, he wrote, 'occurred to me as a result of studying the logarithmic scale on the common slide rule'.[46] The result of Lieutenant Bourdillon's work was the Central Flying School Bombsight (designated C.F.S.) which H.E. Wimperis, designer of the course-setting bombsight, later started 'was then and remained for some years the best bombsight in production anywhere'.[47] (See Figure 2, p. 73).

The sight consisted of a fixed backsight, and vertically beneath it, a fixed foresight, and a movable foresight. The position of the movable foresight was given by an index which moved between two scales; the inner one being marked in heights, the outer one (the time scale) being graduated in seconds. To prepare the sight for bombing the following operations had to be performed. First, it was necessary to discover the direction of the wind, for the sight was designed for use up or down wind. This was done by placing the eye in such a position that the two steering wires (which were in a vertical plane) were coincident and then turning the aircraft until objects on the ground appeared to move directly beneath or parallel to the wires. The direction of the wind would therefore correspond to the course of the aircraft or to the reciprocal of the course; which of the two the pilot would know from the meteorological information he had been given.

The next step was to set the movable foresight to the height of the aircraft on the inner scale, and then to time the passage of an object on the ground from a line of sight formed by the fixed backsight and the movable foresight to a line of sight formed by the fixed backsight and the fixed foresight, which was the vertical. Then the movable foresight was reset so that the number of seconds recorded on the stop watch was set on the time scale. Finally, the bombs were dropped when the target crossed the line of sight

C.F.S.4B BOMBSIGHT

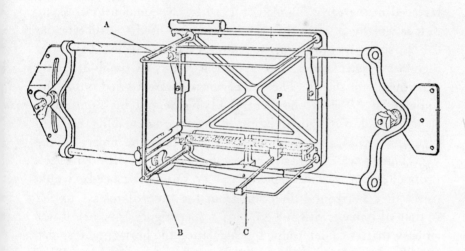

A Fixed Backsight
B Fixed Foresight
C Movable Foresight
P Index between Height Scale and Time Scale

(Figure 2)

formed by the fixed backsight and the movable foresight.[48]

Soon after producing the C.F.S. sight, Lieutenant Bourdillon designed the C.F.S. Trombone sight which was in fact a modification of the ordinary sight. The sight derived its name from the 'trombone' attachment (a sliding backsight) which allowed timing to be done on the actual target, as opposed to some other object. It was intended mainly for use over the sea where the target might well be the only object on which a timing could be made. The trombone sight was issued to the naval squadrons, but remained in service for only a short time, being replaced in the early summer of 1916 by the equal-distance sight.

It is worthy of note that the information used to calibrate the C.F.S. sight was not, as in most previous sights, based on theoretical calculations, but upon the results of bomb-dropping experiments in the air. These experiments were carried out in the summer of 1915 at the Central Flying School by Bourdillon, Henry Tizard, who had lately joined the experimental flight,[49] and Lieutenant G.M.B. Dobson. Broadly speaking, the object of the experiments was to discover how far bombs of different sizes, dropped from various heights and at various airspeeds, would travel in a horizontal direction from the time of release to the instant of impact with the ground.[50] (See Figure 1, p. 42). It was an easy matter to determine by calculation the horizontal distance travelled by a bomb imagined to have fallen in a vacuum. What was not known with any accuracy at that time was the distance which the resistance offered by the air would cause the real bomb to fall short of the 'vacuum bomb'. This distance was known as the ground lag and was measured from the point of impact of a real bomb to the point where it would have fallen in a vacuum. Since therefore the calculations concerning the trajectories of 'vacuum bombs', at given heights and ground speeds, produced invariable results, it will be seen that the information concerning the differences between the trajectories of real and 'vacuum' bombs would provide the data required to calibrate a bombsight with acceptable accuracy.

The main items of equipment used in the experiments were a camera obscura and a wireless transmitter and receiver. The camera obscura was a light excluded hut with a lens of long focus mounted in the roof and directed vertically upwards. While an aircraft was being flown on a straight course directly over the hut a series of photographs was taken at regular time intervals, the shutter of the camera being operated electrically. From these photographs could be determined the track, height and ground speed of the aircraft and the horizontal distance of the aircraft from the camera obscura at any given moment.

When the pilot judged himself to be nearly over the camera he released a bomb. The bomb release mechanism transmitted a wireless signal which was automatically recorded by a syphon recorder, which also recorded each opening of the shutter. It was therefore possible to determine the instant of release in relation to the photographs. Since the track, height and ground speed of the aircraft were known, it was possible to calculate the point of impact of a 'vacuum bomb'. Therefore, the distance between the point of impact of the real bomb and the calculated point of impact of the 'vacuum bomb' gave the ground lag. The two other components of lag — air lag and time lag — were also determined. Air lag, the horizontal distance at any height between the flight path of the 'vacuum bomb' and that of the real bomb, was found by making a correction for wind to the ground lag. Time lag was determined by timing the fall of a bomb from a known height and finding the difference between that time and the time calculated for vacuum conditions.

Thus, for the first time, a bombsight used by the British air services was wholly calibrated upon data obtained by practical experiments. Though the new sight was, as Bourdillon himself realized, a crude device, it fulfilled its function better than any instrument produced up to that time, and for some time after. It was strong enough to withstand the buffeting on an aircraft, was relatively easy to operate and produced acceptably accurate bombing results. After the early models of the sight had been used for experimental purposes, the first operational type, the CFS4, was available early in 1916, and was distributed both to R.F.C. and R.N.A.S. squadrons.

Although naval bombing operations during 1915 had been severely limited by the shortage of aircraft and equipment, there was no lack of ideas at the Admiralty for extending the air offensive as soon as circumstances permitted. The French, too, were forming plans to attack targets in Germany and German occupied territory, but like the Navy, they were compelled to restrict the scope of their operations because of insufficient resources. French plans for strategic bombardment began to take shape in the early months of 1915, by which time it was apparent that the type of warfare developing on the Western Front required vast quantities of munitions.[51] The French General Staff there-fore concentrated its attention on the chemical industry and those other industries engaged in the production of materials essential to the manufacture of powder and explosives.

One target before all others stood out in importance, both because of the vital nature of its products and because of its nearness to French aerodromes, the Badische chemical works (Badische Anilin und Soda Fabrik) at Mannheim. Situated in the great chemical manufacturing area of Mannheim-Ludwigshaven, where the effects of bombing would be felt over a wide area, this factory was, in May 1915, selected as the first objective for attack. Other centres which attracted the attention of the French General Staff, both for their importance and proximity, were the Mauser arms factory at Oberndorf, the powder factory at Rottweil, and to a lesser extent, the Krupp works at Essen.[52]

These plans were however in advance of the aeroplanes needed to carry them out. In the spring of 1915 the French possessed no proper bombing aircraft, and indeed few aircraft capable of carrying a worthwhile bomb-load over the distances involved. Nor was the production of bombers given a high priority, for the General Staff and the Bureau of Aeronautics were pre-occupied with the development of fighting and reconnaissance aircraft. As a result, the French air offensive was delayed, and it was not until the summer of 1916 that attacks on the German munition industry could be given serious consideration.[53]

In October 1915 the French suggested monthly meetings between the British and French air services to discuss questions connected with the supply of aeronautical material.[54] The meetings were agreed upon, but the topics discussed ranged over a far wider field than the supply of materials. It was at one of these early meetings that the French and Admiralty representatives made tentative arrangements for joint bombing operations in the future.[55] The suggestion that the two forces should co-operate in this way first came from the French, but it was taken up and pursued with great enthusiasm by the Admiralty. For the Navy had every reason to look forward to a considerable extension of their offensive operations in 1916. Three new aircraft designed specifically for bombing – from the firms of Sopwith, Handley Page and Short Brothers – were expected to come into squadron service in that year, and plans for their employment were already being considered. The advantages to be gained from the formation of an allied bombing force seemed so attractive to the Admiralty that they were prepared to place the naval bombers under French control.[56]

On 17th December, the meeting between the British and French air services was devoted largely to a discussion of bombing policy. After this meeting, the French Minister of Aviation, who was present at the talks, asked that one of the new C.F.S. bombsights should be supplied to the French air service for trials. The French delegation also visited Brooklands where they saw the new naval bomber, the Sopwith 1½ Strutter, in flight. They were so impressed by its performance that they placed an order for six of these aircraft.[57]

From the beginning, a close co-operation between the French air service and the Admiralty was achieved, and by the end of 1915 a firm understanding was reached that an air offensive against German war industry should be launched as soon as the resources of the two sides permitted. From this agreement there sprang the most imaginative and far-sighted allied plan to exploit one of Germany's outstanding weaknesses — the vulnerability of her chief war industries to attack from the air. Unfortunately, after a promising beginning, the scheme came to nought, but, as will be shown, this failure was brought about, not by faulty planning or execution, but by the opposition of the British military air leaders.

Chapter 3

Growing Military Domination of Air Policy – 1916

By the early part of 1916 there were excellent prospects of a rapid increase in naval bombing strength. The Sopwith Company had begun to manufacture the 1½ Strutter on its own responsibility so that production was well advanced when the official Admiralty order was placed. The French on the other hand were no better placed than they had been in 1915 and still possessed no up-to-date day bombers for long-range work. The Admiralty however were determined to take immediate advantage of the improving situation and began to make preparations for a force of bombers, based at Detling near Maidstone, to operate directly against the German industrial towns of Essen and Düsseldorf. The specific targets were to be the steel manufacturing plants, an important source of material used in the construction of submarines. By the end of February 1916 the first 1½ Strutters had begun to arrive.[1]

Arrangements for the reception of a larger force were soon in hand, but it was not expected that a sufficient number of new aircraft would be available to begin operations before the end of June.[2] There was however one serious obstacle to the proposed operations – the direct route from Detling to the targets lay across part of Holland. It was intended that pilots should be instructed to make a detour to the south to avoid violating Dutch territory, but the Admiralty began to have doubts whether this instruction would be complied with under the stress of operational conditions. Unwilling therefore to risk involving Britain in disputes with a neutral country, the Admiralty decided to abandon the plan and seek employment elsewhere for the growing bomber force.[3]

An approach was at once made to the French to discover whether they still wished an allied bomber force to be formed, and in the event of their being willing to co-operate, to ask that they should make a formal request to the Admiralty to that effect.

I was informed [recorded Captain W.L. Elder, the Admiralty representative] that such a squadron was still desired and that the proposed base from which to commence operations was Luxeuil. Towards the end of May a letter addressed to the Secretary of the Admiralty was received from the French Naval Attache in which the co-operation of the English and French squadron was proposed.[4]

Orders were at once given for No. 3 Wing to be formed under Captain Elder, and by the middle of June the advance naval party had begun to construct a camp at Luxeuil, some twenty-five miles to the north-west of Belfort. The intention at this stage was to build up a wing of sixty aircraft – a number that was to be increased to a hundred in due course.[5]

However, none of these arrangements were put in train until an assurance was received from Sir Douglas Haig that he had no objections to the proposed operations from Luxeuil.[6] In a statement of British bombing policy, issued by G.H.Q. on 3rd June 1916, Haig's attitude to the naval operations could not have been stated in more unequivocal terms:

The C-in-C sees no need to object in any way to long distance bombing being undertaken by the Royal Naval Air Service, with the proviso that any such bombing undertaken in the area behind the German lines in front of the British Army, or necessitating flying over that area, shall be subject to his concurrence. . . . As regards bombing operations undertaken by the Royal Naval Air Service in areas which can in no way affect the British Armies – e.g. in areas in front of the French Army, the C-in-C of the British armies is not concerned and sees no necessity for his concurrence to be obtained.[7]

The categorical nature of this statement is of some significance in the light of Haig's subsequent denunciation of naval bombing policy on the ground that the employment of bombing aircraft in France was a matter for the military authorities.

After the cancellation of the Detling operations the Sopwiths were moved to Manston where the squadrons were to be formed before being despatched to Luxeuil. Preparations at Manston and Luxeuil were soon well in hand, but early in July 1916 came the first of many strokes of ill-fortune which dogged the naval venture until the disbandment of the wing in April 1917. When the air operations of the battle of the Somme began to place a serious strain on the resources of the Flying Corps, Trenchard asked for and was promised sixty of the 1½ Strutter fighters as soon as they were available. To meet this requirement the highest priority was given to the production of fighters. As a result, the output of Sopwith bombers was curtailed and the operations of the Luxeuil force had to be postponed until the autumn of 1916.[8]

But the Luxeuil wing was not the only cause of frustration to the Admiralty's strategic policy. In June the long-range bombing operations of the Dunkirk squadrons were suspended by order of the Vice-Admiral, Dover Patrol. The progress made by this force in its offensive against the German naval bases had been slow and disappointing. During the first year of the war long-range operations had been severely restricted by the lack of suitable aircraft, but in 1916 another factor began to influence the employment of air forces in this theatre. Unlike No. 3 Wing, which was directly controlled by the Admiralty, the Dunkirk force came under the orders of the Vice-Admiral, Dover Patrol, Admiral R.H. Bacon, whose ideas on the use of aircraft were at variance with the policy being developed by the Air Department of the Admiralty. When in a report of 1st June 1916 Captain C.L. Lambe, commander of the Dunkirk force, suggested that conditions of air warfare were then changing rapidly and would probably change with equal rapidity in the near future,[9] Admiral Bacon denied that this was so.

> It is not [he wrote] the conditions of aerial warfare that have changed, but our airmen are beginning to learn that warfare in the air, to be useful, has to be entirely subservient to warfare on land — or at sea.[10]

Convinced of the correctness of this doctrine, Admiral Bacon attached no great importance to the creation of a strategic bomber force. The air force under his command was intended to be employed primarily as an auxiliary to naval operations. If bombing attacks on the German bases coincided with the requirements of the naval war, then they would be undertaken; but he did not subscribe to the view that such attacks would by themselves produce worthwhile results.

Admiral Bacon was doubtless correct in his decision to suspend bombing operations from June 1916, on the grounds that the bombing force then available was too weak to inflict appreciable damage on the German bases and that light sporadic attacks would merely alert the enemy's defences and perhaps bring retaliatory raids against the allied bases around Dunkirk.[11] But at the same time his general policy retarded the development of a bomber force of adequate strength. He gave orders that every available aircraft that could be fitted out for fighting duties should be prepared for that purpose in readiness for his proposed naval operations.[12] And he was prepared to lift the ban on bombing operations so that his squadrons could assist the Flying Corps in bombing tactical objectives during the battle of the Somme.[13] Further, he was willing to provide this kind of support for the Army whenever he could reasonably do so. Thus the Dunkirk force was committed to a wider range of operations than its strength would allow it adequately to perform, with the result that long-range bombing never received the necessary equipment and personnel to carry it out effectively.

Meanwhile, the first half of 1916 was a period of increasing difficulties for the Royal Flying Corps. The shortsightedness of the military air policy was for the first time beginning to be felt. Throughout the previous year the inadequacy of most types of military aircraft for war operations had been concealed because the enemy had possessed few fighting machines capable of exploiting that weakness. But the situation changed drastically in the early part of 1916 with the appearance in numbers of the Fokker armed with a machine-gun firing through the arc of the airscrew. Immediately, R.F.C. losses – especially of the slow, almost defenceless B.E.2's – began to rise steeply. The Corps was now made to pay dearly for its failure to anticipate the need for an effective fighting machine.

But more serious, and less easily reparable, was the damage caused by the policy of placing great dependence on the range of B.E.2 aircraft for 'all-round' duties. The most 'popular' of these was the B.E.2c for which large orders were placed early in the war. There were considerable delays in production and the output of this type did not reach its peak until the end of 1915, by which time the growth of air fighting had rendered it obsolete. Yet by the middle of 1916 nearly fifty per cent of the total number of aeroplanes in use by the R.F.C. in France were B.E.2c's.[14] But the enthusiasm of the authorities for this aircraft was not shared by the crews who flew in it. The comments of Cecil Lewis are typical of many that were later recorded.

If there was ever an aeroplane unsuited for active service, it was the B.E.2c. The pilot sat slightly aft of the main planes and had a fair view above and below, except where the lower plane obscured the ground forward; but the observer, who sat in front of him, could see practically nothing, for he was wedged under the small centre section, with the plane above, another below, and bracing wires all round. He carried a gun for defence purposes; but he could not fire it forward, because of the propeller. Backwards, the centre-section struts, wires, and tail plane cramped his style.[15]

The difficult situation in France quickly reacted on another major weakness of the Flying Corps — that of training. In spite of the fact that the war was nearing the end of its second year in July 1916, the Corps had not yet evolved a training system adequate to meet the requirements of an operational force. Unlike the Navy, which provided appropriate training for the type of aircraft the pilot was intended to fly on the squadron,[16] the Army gave only the most elementary training to all pilots before posting them to a squadron. As losses became heavier, the calls on the training schools to provide greater numbers of pilots became more insistent. Consequently, training standards were further reduced, and many pilots despatched to France were hardly competent to fly the aircraft in which they were to operate over the front. A total of some twenty flying hours, of which about two-thirds would be solo, was perhaps the average experience of a newly qualified pilot on arrival at a squadron.[17] Trenchard often wrote complaining that pilots sent to France were inadequately trained,[18] but he seemed unaware that his constant demands for more and more pilots to maintain his offensive policy were in large measure responsible for lowering the standards of training.

While the R.F.C. in France was beginning to feel the full effects of its lack of planning and the R.N.A.S. was laying the foundations of the first ever strategic bombing force, Sir David Henderson in London had launched an attack against naval air policy. This led, first, to a dispute between the War Office and the Admiralty and, ultimately, to the disbandment of the Luxeuil naval wing and to the complete suspension of all strategic operations.

Henderson's attack began with a memorandum to the Joint War Air Committee, the body set up in February 1915, under the chairmanship of Lord Derby, 'to collaborate in and to co-ordinate the question of supplies and design of material for the Naval and Military Air Services'.[19] This memorandum, dated 4th February 1916, complained that the Admiralty was using unfair methods to secure its own requirements of aeronautical supplies. He cited the example of high-powered engines of which there was a severe shortage. At the beginning of the war the Admiralty had, he stated, been given priority in the supply of high-powered engines because of the extra power needed for seaplanes. Now, however, the R.F.C. had urgent need of such engines for land aeroplanes but were experiencing the greatest difficulty in obtaining supplies because the Admiralty was still placing orders with firms which the two air services had by mutual agreement allotted to the R.F.C. The reason for this harmful competition for aeronautical material was, he contended, the lack of any instruction defining the particular duties to be undertaken by each service in war; with the result that some duties 'such as long-range offensive operations are being prepared for by both Services, and there is a grave possibility of duplication and consequent waste'. He therefore suggested that the duties of each service should be defined and stated in order of importance and, in the light of these decisions, the best distribution of available material arrived at.[20] His object in making this suggestion was patent. He hoped to obtain a ruling that the R.F.C. would have sole responsibility for land operations, in which case the naval supplies of aircraft and aero-engines which were then being assembled for strategic bombing would be re-allocated to the Flying Corps.

A second document sent by the War Office to the Joint War Air Committee, on 2nd March 1916, detailed the duties that should be undertaken by the R.F.C., and was more specific about the responsibility for strategic bombing.

The Royal Flying Corps must also be prepared to undertake

long-range offensive operations against military or national objectives. Such operations, if undertaken by land aeroplanes, will almost invariably be based on a theatre occupied or controlled by land forces, and should therefore be undertaken by the Royal Flying Corps.

A further list of Flying Corps duties followed, and then a somewhat unexpected observation.

It is impossible to forecast with accuracy the extent to which the Royal Flying Corps will be able to fulfil satisfactorily its duties without taking into consideration the extent to which the Royal Naval Air Service will assist in, or will interfere with, the development of the military wing.

It was soon made clear that it was interference that was to be expected, and that the source of that interference would be the supply of aeronautical material 'which brings the Navy into direct competition with the Army in every respect'.[21]

Not unnaturally, a statement couched in such terms caused deep resentment at the Admiralty.

It appears, [wrote Sir Henry Jackson, the First Sea Lord] to be worded in a rather offensive manner, with the object of preventing the Navy developing its air service to its fullest extent, on the plea that it may interfere with the R.F.C. It is a case of military convenience versus naval efficiency and I cannot imagine any independent judge accepting such an argument and it must be resisted in every way and referred to the Board if necessary.[22]

The Admiralty reply to these allegations was made in a strongly worded note by the naval members of the Joint War Air Committee. In it they stated that much had been made of 'overlapping and interference in design, supply contract work etc' but that no real evidence had been produced to substantiate these statements. It seemed to them that the charge of overlapping was merely 'a pretext for demanding Naval material'. It was true, they admitted, that the Admiralty had not always been able to accede to the full demands of the War Office for the output of firms introduced by the Navy into the aircraft industry, but that hardly constituted interference.

Regarding the actual shortage in the requirements for the Army, [the note continued] it is not desired to open up the question whether the Royal Aircraft Factory has fulfilled expectations as regards either engines or machines and whether in reality this is not the crux of the whole question.

The note emphasized that the Admiralty would do all in its power to help the Army to overcome its difficulties, even if that involved postponing naval long-distance bombing operations. The naval members ended by stating that the two air services should co-operate fully in bringing about the defeat of the enemy, and that because of this overriding consideration, the question of what duties should be allocated to each service should be left until after the war.[23]

However much the Admiralty might have wished to avoid an open dispute with the War Office, the issue raised was one which Lord Derby, chairman of the Joint War Air Committee, felt he could not ignore. Already convinced that the deep differences of opinion between the two air services rendered it impossible for his committee, as then constituted, to frame a joint air policy, Lord Derby sent a minute to the Prime Minister suggesting what action should be taken to remedy the situation. He recommended, first, that the Government should nominate the specific functions of the two air services, and secondly, that the powers and functions of the Joint War Air Committee should be extended 'or that a fresh Committee be formed with full powers to order and allot aircraft as may be required by the two Departments concerned, their decision in such matters being considered as final'.[24]

The direction in which Lord Derby's thought was moving at this time may be gauged by a memorandum on the principles governing the use of aircraft in war which he circulated to the members of the Joint War Air Committee. The main idea propounded in this memorandum, whose author was not named, was that 'the air force which acts with the Army is really part of that Army and should be organized and controlled as such . . .' and 'similarly the air force which acts with the Fleet is really part of that Fleet and should be organized and controlled as such'. In short, the primary functions of aeroplanes were to operate either with the Army or the Navy. Consequently, any diversion of air power from these two functions was a waste of effort.

> Opinion has been misled [stated the memorandum] by the air raids against towns, munition factories, aerodromes, etc, which are really secondary operations . . . . The false ideal engendered by basing policy on the secondary operations instead of on the primary tends not only to mistaken strategy but to the production of . . . air machines unsound in principle. The force produced in view of the primary operations will probably cover the needs of the secondary ones.

Stated in broad terms, the thesis of the memorandum was that air power was primarily a tactical weapon and that it could make no contribution to the overall strategy for winning the war.[25]

Before forwarding the minute referred to above to the Prime Minister, Lord Derby first circulated a draft of it among the members of the Joint War Air Committee. Not unnaturally, the naval members were quick to perceive that the recommendation that the Government should make a decision as to the duties each service should perform was putting the cart before the horse. What should be asked, they thought, was what types of operations should be given the highest priority and which of the two services was better equipped to carry them out. They believed that 'it would be a retrograde movement, and cause endless delay, to refer to the Government and ask for policy. A far better course is to evolve a Policy, and where we differ, ask for a definite decision on definite points in question'.

In any case, they did not agree that wide differences of opinion existed between the two services. The only significant difference of opinion so far as they were concerned was as to which service should undertake long-range bombing operations. And even that was not as serious as it might appear, because in view of the importance of this type of bombing, both services should join together in carrying it out. But since the Flying Corps was not at that time in a position to undertake long-range operations, it had already been agreed, the naval members pointed out, 'that the Naval programme for long distance raiding should not be delayed until the R.F.C. were ready to co-operate. . . '. Consequently, they thought that the difficulties of formulating a viable policy were exaggerated in the minute, and were convinced that such difficulties as arose could be overcome by discussion within the framework of the existing committee.[26]

This argument did not however alter Lord Derby's conviction that the Joint War Air Committee did not possess the necessary powers to carry out its appointed functions, and on 3rd April he sent a letter of resignation to the Prime Minister. In this letter he stated that since the Committee possessed no executive power and no authority it could not resolve the conflicting ideas on policy which existed between the two services.

It appears to me, [he wrote] to be quite impossible to bring the two Wings closer together than they are at the present moment, unless and until the whole system of the Air Service is changed and they are amalgamated into one service as personally I consider they ultimately must be. To make this great change would be a difficult and lengthy operation in peace time. I am inclined to think it would be practically impossible in war time . . . .

* * *

In due course, a new body, the Air Board, was set up and Lord
Curzon was appointed president. The main functions of the Air
Board were to discuss matters of general air policy, to make
recommendations concerning the types of aircraft required by the
two services and to organize and co-ordinate the supply of
material so as to obviate competition between the two departments.[28] Yet the Air Board was no better placed than the Joint
War Air Committee to enforce its decisions. It had no executive
powers and lacked the authority to lay down policy which would
determine the types of aircraft to be ordered.[29] However, there is
little doubt that if these two bodies had possessed the powers they
desired they would have used them to compel the Navy to fall into
line with military policy. For it is clear from the records of their
meetings that they were in general agreement with military
thought, accepting that the primary function of aircraft was to act
in direct support of military and naval operations and that the vast
expenditure of air resources on the Western Front was vital to the
successful conduct of the war.[30]

Consequently, the plans put forward by the Admiralty received
less than a fair hearing. When the naval staff proposed the
formation of a force of strategic bombers, the scheme was judged,
not by its probable effectiveness against the enemy war effort, but
by the effect it was likely to have on the build-up of the air force
on the Western Front. The leaders of the R.F.C. had no quarrel
with this attitude, for they now realized that if they were to
continue to increase their air support for the Army they would
have to secure a considerable proportion of the equipment and
aircraft which the Navy was providing for its own squadrons. In
practical terms, this meant restricting the scope of naval air
operations as much as possible. At first, Sir David Henderson
contented himself with asking for a definition of the precise

functions of each service, in the expectation that such a ruling would lead to a curtailment of naval activities, especially over land. But when this failed to produce the desired ruling, and the Armiralty continued to pursue their strategic bombing campaign, he attacked the naval schemes at the meetings of the Air Board, and in concert with Trenchard, induced Haig to write a strong letter of protest.

The dispute between the two air services was brought to a head by the visit to London, in October 1916, of Colonel Barrés, of the French air service, an ardent supporter of strategic bombing. The purpose of this visit was to seek British support for an extension of the air attacks against Germany. Though he intended to present his views both to the Admiralty and to the War Office, it was from the Admiralty alone that he expected to receive a sympathetic hearing. In France, Trenchard had made clear to him the Army's attitude towards long-range bombing.[31] At his first meeting with the British air leaders Colonel Barrés made his appeal for greater co-operation between the two countries.

The gist of his argument was that in addition to the bombing of enemy industrial centres the Allies should embark on a campaign of reprisal raids. This was the only effective answer, he believed, to the German Zeppelin and submarine campaigns. His proposal was 'that immediately after a Zeppelin raid (on the same day if possible) a raid on German open towns should be made, and similar raids should be carried out immediately after a submarine outrage'. The raids must be made with sufficient power 'to make the Germans realize that whatever advantages they might gain by Zeppelin and Submarine attacks were far outweighed by the disadvantages of having their towns subjected to allied raids'. But the deterrent effect was not the most important advantage Colonel Barrés expected to gain. He believed that 'the end of the war would be brought about by the effective bombing of open towns'. To achieve this, a larger bomber force would be needed, and therefore greater numbers of aero-engines. Colonel Barrés urged the British air services to lose no time in placing orders in France for Hispano-Suiza and Clerget engines.[32]

Though not accepting Colonel Barrés views on the bombing of open towns, as their subsequent policy showed, the Admiralty received with enthusiasm the proposal to extend the Anglo-French bombing operations. They therefore directed a memorandum to the Air Board stating that they wished to co-operate in the French plan and suggesting that   .

> . . . it should be definitely laid down that the Navy should keep an effective force of at least two hundred bombers in France (to include Dunkirk), and if this policy commends itself, it is considered that orders for one thousand Hispanos and one thousand Clergets would not be excessive for the R.N.A.S. alone.[33]

The reaction of the War Office was not unexpected. In a memorandum dated 31st October, Sir David Henderson completely rejected the idea of an air force containing the proportion of bombers to fighters which the naval scheme implied.

> Therefore, I cannot accept the Admiralty proposal that two hundred Naval aeroplanes should be devoted to bombing in France. It is an unimportant duty compared with fighting or reconnaissance, nor does it seem to fall in any way within the sphere of Naval duties.

As in his previous opposition to Admiralty policy, he stressed the importance of making a definite decision concerning the duties and requirements of the two air services.

> No material, [he concluded] should be wasted by being used for purposes of secondary importance; the allotment of all available material should therefore be undertaken afresh, during the winter, irrespective of the original source of the orders under the present competitive method.[34]

Trenchard too contributed his arguments against the Admiralty proposals. He stated that the policy of the Commander-in-Chief was, as he understood it, to give first priority to artillery spotting and reconnaissance aircraft. But if these aircraft were to carry out their duties with the minimum of interference from enemy machines a large number of fighting aircraft would be required, and only when these had been supplied should long-distance bombing machines be provided in large numbers. 'I would point out,' he warned, 'that if the Navy obtain large numbers of engines and machines that the Army require, the effect will be seriously felt in the Spring.' He also reminded the Air Board that he had, at a meeting of that body on 9th June, put forward a request from the Commander-in-Chief 'that ten long distance bombing squadrons (nearly two hundred machines) should be provided for the Army after the other machines had been secured'. In view of the fact that these squadrons had not yet been provided, any engines and machines which were available should go to the Army.[35]

Trenchard also appealed to Haig to throw the weight of his authority into the attack on the naval plan,[36] and on 1st November, the day on which Henderson was, for the first time, stating his true opinion of the value of strategic operations before the Air Board, a strong letter of protest was despatched from G.H.Q. France to the War Office. In this letter Haig attacked the Admiralty plans on the grounds that they were based on mistaken air policy and would lead to an allocation of materials for purposes of secondary importance.

As regards air policy, some of the views put forward by Colonel Barrés appear to me to be based more on enthusiasm for his own particular service than on sound military judgement. For example, I observe that he is reported to have said that in his opinion 'the end of the war would be brought about by the effective bombing of open towns'. In this, as in various other statements attributed to him, he claims entirely too much for the effects of bombing.

There was only one way, Sir Douglas Haig believed, to bring about a successful end to the war and that was to obtain a 'decisive victory over the enemy's forces in the field'. In any case, he did not suppose that the Government would view with any more favour than he did 'the bombing of open towns merely for the purpose of terrorizing the civil population'. In spite of his previous agreement to the formation of the naval wing at Luxeuil, he now contended that 'the employment of bombing machines in France is . . . primarily even if not entirely, a military question . . .' and protested strongly against 'any interference by the naval authorities with the British land forces in such questions'. With regard to the supply of air material, the C-in-C stated that the units working with the land forces should have first priority. The only valuable type of bombing was that directed against tactical objectives to influence the issue of a battle.

> Long range bombing [he continued] as a means of defeating the enemy is entirely secondary to the above requirements. Its success is far more doubtful, and, even when successful, both theory and practice go to show that usually its results are comparatively unimportant.

He concluded with the warning that if his own requirements were not first met, the provision of aircraft for the Admiralty 'for work on the fronts of the French or Belgian armies in France amounts to very serious interference with the British land forces, and may compromise the success of my operations'.[37]

At a meeting of the Air Board on 1st November, when the question of long-range bombing operations was discussed at length, the naval members explained and defended Admiralty policy. Rear-Admiral F.C.T. Tudor, the Third Sea Lord,[38] stated that it was not the intention of the Admiralty to suggest that these operations should be carried out by the R.N.A.S. rather than by the R.F.C. The fact was that the Admiralty, which attached the greatest importance to such operations, had agreed to undertake them because the Army had not possessed the necessary aircraft to do so.

In reply, Lord Curzon said that he and his civilian colleagues at the Air Board had discussed the problem and had agreed that these operations properly fell within the province of the R.F.C. But since the R.N.A.S. alone had suitable aircraft for long-distance work, the Air Board had confined themselves to discussing the policy which should govern the Admiralty's bombing programme. Now however the Admiralty were contemplating a considerable extension of their bombing operations – a policy which entailed the placing of large orders for aero-engines – and although the Air Board had no authority to give a decision on this policy, it was their duty to express an opinion on this matter to the War Committee.

Sir David Henderson then made clear the true feelings of the General Staff concerning long-range bombing.

> The C-in-C France, the C.I.G.S. and the Military represent-
> atives on the Air Board were in agreement that the really
> important thing was to maintain a force, first for fighting in
> the air; secondly, for reconnaissance, thirdly, for bombing in
> connection with military operations, and fourthly, from time
> to time as occasion offered, for long-range bombing. They
> considered that to tie up aircraft for long-range bombing
> alone was a waste of material.

He reminded the Board that Sir Douglas Haig had asked for sixty-six squadrons, of which fourteen were for bombing; but confessed that he was unable to see how the sixty-six squadrons could be maintained at the same time as the two hundred bombers proposed by the Admiralty. Then he returned to the question of the duties to be performed by each service. He said he 'had never departed from the principle that the R.F.C. should be responsible for aerial operations on land', and that, 'he had assented to the R.N.A.S. going on with long-range bombing operations, but most unwillingly'. When Admiral Tudor suggested that every one of our machines employed on bombing withdrew three enemy aircraft from the Front, Henderson denied that this was so. 'In any case,' he said, 'the Army preferred to get the enemy fighters at the Front and destroy them, rather than have them occupied on defence service at Home.' In reply to Lord Sydenham's enquiry as to whether the C-in-C would remove the bombers of the Luxeuil force if they were placed at his disposal, Sir David Henderson replied that he certainly would. In his view 'General Trenchard would bring them to the Somme, take the engines out of them and put them into fighting machines and would confine himself to bombing behind the enemy's lines as at present'.[39]

When Lord Curzon despatched his promised communication to the War Committee, on 9th November, he attached to it a copy of Sir Douglas Haig's letter which he had then received. According to his stated intention, he dealt first with the difference of opinion as to which service should undertake long-range bombing, and secondly, with the relative importance of bombing operations in view of the fact that the R.F.C. considered them of secondary value.[40] Like the chairman of the Joint War Air Committee, Lord Curzon was more concerned to arrive at a proper division of duties than to examine and give an opinion on the various policies put forward. He took for granted that the military estimates of the number of squadrons required on the Western Front were correct and that the air war on that front was being conducted in the most effective way possible. On the other hand, he did not consider the possible advantages of an allied offensive against German war industry, nor did he comment on the effects of the Zeppelin raids on Britain. It was therefore a foregone conclusion that he would recommend a limitation of naval operations. Recording the final decision of the Air Board he wrote:

We think that, as a matter of principle, the only long-range air operations to be undertaken by the Navy should be such as can be conducted from a naval base, whether on our shores, the shores of the enemy where not in our military occupation, or at sea. We hold further that no naval air operations should be undertaken over a territory occupied by, or in front of, British military forces without the previous knowledge and concurrence of the General Officer commanding those forces. We do not recede from the view that a long range offensive is in itself a most desirable thing and should be systematically pursued when the force is available for that purpose. But we think that the military and not the naval authorities are the proper judge of such a situation.[41]

As has been shown, the opposition to the naval policy was completely successful and soon afterwards the Luxeuil force was disbanded. It must however be stated that the Admiralty case never received a fair hearing and the effect produced on the enemy by the naval bombing was deliberately underestimated. Quite unjustly, the Official Historian blamed Haig for the opposition to strategic operations.

There is not much doubt that Sir Douglas Haig objected to an independent naval air detachment operating from French soil against what he considered to be military targets.[42]

Those who were responsible escaped censure. For it is certain that Trenchard had objected from the start to the formation of the Luxeuil wing,[43] and Henderson himself had stated at the Air Board meeting of 1st November that he had given his assent to the naval operations with great reluctance.[44] It must therefore have been Haig who originally made the decision to approve the naval bombing plans and who authorized a statement to that effect in the G.H.Q. directive of 3rd June 1916.[45]

Haig's letter of 1st November is another matter. Clearly, it was written after Trenchard had represented in the strongest terms the effects which he believed the proposed extension of naval bombing would produce on the military air situation. Equally

G

clearly, Haig felt he could not afford to ignore the views put forward by his chief air adviser. 'The crisp style of this letter is unmistakably Haig's,' commented Andrew Boyle, 'though the facts and arguments are just as clearly Trenchard's.'[46]

* * *

During 1916, the work initiated by the Admiralty to improve the efficiency of bombsights began to produce results. Early in that year, the Navy introduced into service the equal-distance sight designed by Warrant Officer F.W. Scarff. (See Fig. 3, p. 101) The main feature of his sight was that it could be 'set' for use by timing on the actual target, a procedure that was impossible when timing was done back to the vertical, as in the case of the standard C.F.S.4 sight.[47] It could be used to great advantage over the sea where the target itself, a surface vessel or a submarine, for instance, would probably be the first object to be sighted after a flight of some duration. The equal-distance sight, which was produced in several forms, was based on the principle that when an aircraft's ground speed remains constant the distance which the aircraft covers over the ground in any given time also remains constant. To operate the sight a special reversible stop watch was required. When the watch was started, a single hand moved over a dial graduated in heights, each height mark being placed at the number of seconds corresponding to the time of fall of a bomb. When the watch lever was pressed a second time the hand went into reverse and moved back to zero at the same rate. On the rim of the watch there was a movable indicator which could be set to the desired duration on the height scale marked on the watch face.

The sight itself consisted of a fixed backsight, and two movable foresights which were attached to a vertical slide which moved horizontally along a height scale. The sight was ready for use when the slide had been set at the approximate height of the aircraft. On the run-up to the target, made either up or down wind, the pilot, having levelled the sight, set the movable indicator on the stop watch to the height shown on the altimeter. He then sighted the target along the backsight and upper foresight, and when the target came on he started the stop watch and at once took sight along the backsight and lower foresight. As soon as the target crossed this line of sight he set the watch in reverse, and when the hand was about to coincide with the movable indicator he released the bomb. It will be seen that the sight was so designed that the time taken on the second run, that is, when the watch hand was in reverse, was equal to the time on the first run minus the number of seconds for a bomb to fall from the height at which the aircraft was flying.[48]

The centre of naval experimental work was the R.N.A.S. station on the Isle of Grain where, among other things, experiments were being carried out to discover the time lag of various bombs.[49] But the most important discoveries were made as a result of a series of experiments conducted by Lieutenant H.E. Wimperis, in the summer of 1916, at the Rossington Main Colliery near Doncaster. Here, bombs of all sizes were dropped down a mineshaft 2,700 feet deep. The instants of release and impact were recorded electrically by a chronograph so that the actual time of fall was recorded with great accuracy. The difference between this time and the time calculated for vacuum conditions gave the time lag. Equally important, the experiments revealed, for the first time, the 'fall' characteristics of the small bombs. These findings enabled Lieutenant Wimperis to recommend that slight modifications should be made to the shape of the 65 lb. and 100 lb. bombs so that their passage through the air would be speeded up to the point at which their trajectory approximated to that of the 112 lb. and 500 lb. bombs. The experiments also showed that the 180, 250 and 550 lb. bombs belonged to a faster group which required to be dropped about one second earlier than the slower group.[50] The discovery that the standard bombs could be divided into two categories in respect of their 'fall' characteristics made possible the more accurate calibration of bombsights.

In the Flying Corps, Lieutenant Bourdillon produced an

improved version of the C.F.S.4 sight, and this was designated C.F.S.4B.[51] The principle on which the C.F.S.4 was based was also employed to design a sight for use on those aircraft such as the R.E.7, the Martinsyde and the Sopwith 1½ Strutter which, because of their fuselage design, could not be fitted with standard sights. The sight evolved was of the periscope type and was used with a fair degree of success on the R.E.7 and the Martinsyde. It was however a failure on the 1½ Strutter because the considerable quantity of oil thrown out by the engine obstructed the sighting device. The periscope sight incorporated an optical system which enabled the pilot to view the ground ahead of the aircraft without leaning out of the cockpit. The sighting was done by means of a crosswire which was placed at one of the focal planes of the sight so that the wire and the view of the ground were in focus together. The position of the crosswire was set by rotating a drum which moved across a scale graduated in feet on the upper side and in seconds on the lower side. The basic operation to prepare the sight for bombing was a timed run. First, the drum was set to the height of the aircraft, and when the object selected for timing crossed the wire a stop watch was started. Then the crosswire was moved back to the vertical by turning the drum to the stop position, and as soon as the object crossed the wire for the second time the watch was stopped. Finally, the drum was rotated until the recorded time was set on the time scale, and when the target crossed the wire the bomb was released.[52]

In 1916 too Bourdillon introduced a new sight, the Low Height Sight C.F.S.7, but this instrument represented no advance in bombsight design. Though simpler to operate, it was in fact less accurate than previous standard sights, since the use of a stop watch to determine ground speed was virtually out of the question at the low altitudes — a thousand feet and less — for which the sight was constructed. The main setting on the sight depended wholly upon the pilot's ability to estimate his ground speed correctly. Unlike other sights, which were fitted to the fuselage horizontal to the aircraft's normal flying position, the C.F.S.7 was

R.N.A.S. EQUAL-DISTANCE BOMBSIGHT

P Backsight
Q Upper Foresight
R Lower Foresight
Face C of carrier D set against horizontal height scale H

(Figure 3)

fixed at an angle of approximately 40 degrees to the horizontal. The sight had two discs set together: the inner one, which was rigidly attached to the frame of the sight, had engraved on its circumference a scale in miles per hour; the outer one, which was movable and controlled the position of the sighting wires, was marked with a scale of heights. Between the two discs was a movable pointer which was set against the inner disc to the estimated ground-speed. The outer disc was then turned until the height of the aircraft was shown against the pointer. The sight was then set, and as soon as the target was seen along the sighting wires the bomb was released.[53]

By the autumn of 1916, however, the sights described above had been rendered obsolete by the developments in air warfare which had taken place during the battle of the Somme. In particular, enemy defences against air attack had greatly improved. Pilots on bombing missions were more frequently attacked by enemy fighters, and, especially in the vicinity of important targets, encountered heavier and more accurate fire from the ground. In these circumstances, it is not surprising that they found the existing sights, which required the use of a stop watch, unnecessarily difficult to operate. There was a clear need, therefore, for a sight which could be set without a timed run. Fortunately, a replacement for the standard sight was soon to be available. Before the end of 1916, H.E. Wimperis had produced the first of his three sights, each of which proved to be a notable improvement upon the previous sights of its type.[54]

Chapter 4

Naval Strategic Air Operations,
October 1916 – March 1918

The formation and organization of the naval bombing wing was from the beginning beset by misfortunes. Soon after the initial arrangements had been made for the reception of the squadrons at Luxeuil, General Trenchard made an urgent request for extra fighting aircraft to co-operate with the Army in the action on the Somme. The request was forwarded through the Air Board to the Admiralty, who responded by diverting no less than sixty Sopwith 1½ Strutter fighters to the Flying Corps. As a result of this action, the production of the bomber version of the 1½ Strutter, the type which was to have been almost exclusively supplied to the new bombing wing, was seriously retarded. Deliveries of the Sopwith bomber to No. 3 Wing were therefore delayed, and it was not until October that the naval force possessed a sufficient number of aircraft to begin operations.[1] For with the full concurrence of the French, the Admiralty had issued strict instructions that no operations should be undertaken until the force had assembled sufficient strength to make them effective. Both the British and French authorities believed that weak attacks on important objectives would serve merely to put the enemy on his guard.[2]

The immediate effect of the diversion of aircraft to the Flying Corps was to prevent the naval squadrons from operating during the months when weather conditions would be most favourable for long-distance operations. The long-term effects were, however, more serious, for the shortage of aircraft disrupted the French as well as the British preparations. Since the Admiralty had revived the idea of a joint bombing campaign, the French had made clear that their own contribution to the offensive would depend largely upon a supply of suitable aircraft from Britain.

At a joint aviation conference in London, on 4th July 1916, the French delegation were frank about their deficiencies. They admitted that neither of their standard day bombers, the Maurice Farman F40 and the Caudron twin-engined G4, were really adequate for the operations that both sides had in mind. They placed their reliance mainly upon the 1½ Strutter which they considered an excellent type for long-distance day operations.[3] The Admiralty accepted the situation and in fact agreed that the French should be supplied with one-third of the Sopwiths which were delivered to Luxeuil. Thus, the initial loss of so many aircraft to the Flying Corps not only delayed the start of the naval operations but also reduced the effectiveness of the French bomber force, and placed the whole Allied campaign in jeopardy.

After the arrival of naval equipment and personnel at Luxeuil, the French were not unnaturally perturbed by the slow growth of the operational force, and pressed Captain Elder, the commander of the Wing, for tangible proof of the British intention to co-operate. On 22nd July 1916, Captain Elder reported to the Admiralty that by the end of that month no more than six 1½ Strutters would be ready, and even these would not be equipped with bombsights and stop watches.[4] A month later he again wrote to the Admiralty concerning the strength of the force. Only thirteen Sopwiths were at that time, he stated, ready for active service. The two 250 horse-power Shorts were both out of action and the four Breguets which had been delivered were not 'at least in their present state of armament, suitable for such raids as the French contemplate'. He pointed out that the delays in delivering aircraft to Luxeuil were proving more serious than he had been led to believe and were creating a difficult situation for the British force. The French hoped to have a force of fifty aircraft ready in two weeks' time and looked to the British to provide a force of comparable strength. The French, he stated, could not understand why the British 'were not in a position to give them substantial help, or at least help bearing some relation to the scale of our preparations here'.[5]

Nor had the situation improved much by the end of October. By that time, Captain Elder was able to estimate the likely development of the force during the coming months and compare it with the programme which had originally been approved. He wrote to the Admiralty on 22nd October:

> It would appear that the maximum number of 1½ Strutters likely to be ready by the end of February will be sixty-three, instead of an originally anticipated hundred by the end of the year.

He was of the opinion that 'this number of 1½ Strutters will not be even sufficient for the English force at Luxeuil' for 'the French have been definitely promised one-third of the machines sent to this aerodrome'.[6]

Another factor which aggravated an already difficult situation was the exceptionally bad weather which seriously curtailed operations during the winter months. Luxeuil lies in an area where in normal years winters are severe, and low clouds and mists persist for long periods from late autumn to early spring. But during the period of No. 3 Wing's operations, from October 1916 to April 1917, weather conditions were much worse than usual. During the autumn of 1916, heavy clouds along the routes to more distant targets frequently caused operations to be cancelled or take-off to be delayed so long that only the minimum of daylight was left to enable the bombers to return to base before darkness. Fogs too were a constant hazard, and the valleys in which may of the nearer targets lay were often shrouded in mist for considerable periods. Though weather conditions had begun to improve by the beginning of February, operations were still most difficult to carry out, as Captain Elder described.

During February [he wrote] the weather cleared considerably and on four days it was fine and clear. The temperature,
however, was very low and it was possible to carry out only
one raid in this month. The hangars at Ochey were not
heated and the cold was so intense that even the oil in the
Clerget engines froze. Every device was used to keep the
machines sufficiently warm for flying, but it was found
impossible to keep more than a very few ready at one time.
At the end of February, the weather became milder but
unfortunately the fog and mist increased over the objectives
so much that pilots had to return from raids without
dropping their bombs. Attempts were also made to set out on
raids but owing to the weather conditions the machines were
forced to return without crossing the lines.[7]

In 1917 further demands from the Army for aircraft and
personnel increased the operational difficulties of the wing. At the
end of January Captain Elder was instructed to transfer nine of his
best pilots to Dunkirk where they were required to assist Flying
Corps operations. Naturally, the withdrawal of the most skilful
pilots reduced the general efficiency of the force. In particular, the
progress which was being made to achieve effective formation
flying, the bombers' main defence against enemy fighters, received
a severe setback. The introduction at one time of so many
replacement pilots necessitated special training to achieve an
acceptable standard of formation flying. Though this shock was
successfully absorbed, it was in fact the beginning of the end. On
7th March, nineteen more pilots, six 1½ Strutter fighters and one
hundred ratings were posted to Dunkirk. Again the flights had to
be reorganized, but in spite of the difficulties created, three
long-distance raids were carried out during the month.[8] By this
time the weather was improving and the prospect of launching a
full-scale offensive was in view. Then the final blow fell. On 25th
March the Admiralty despatched a telegram instructing Captain
Elder to close down the wing.[9] And so the boldest, and perhaps

the most successful, experiment in the use of air power during the war was brought to an end.

Without doubt, No. 3 Wing was sacrificed to enable Trenchard to throw even greater numbers of aircraft into the coming air battles on the Western Front. On 11th December 1916 he had appeared in person before the Air Board to state that he would have neither sufficient aircraft nor spares for the following year and to ask for four fully equipped naval squadrons and 150 aero-engines from those being supplied to the Admiralty. The Air Board put this 'request' to the Admiralty who agreed to assist. The effects which this transfer of aircraft and equipment produced on the R.N.A.S. were summed up by the Official Historian.

> They entailed considerable reductions in the naval air stations at home. The Eastchurch War Flight was abolished and that at Manston reduced by one third. Ultimately, also, it was found compulsory to disband No. 3 Naval (Bombing) Wing at Luxeuil. Three of the four naval fighting squadrons had joined the Royal Flying Corps by the end of March 1917, and the fourth arrived in the middle of May.[10]

The agreement between the Admiralty and the French for a joint air offensive was based on the understanding that the naval force should be placed under the operational control of the French.[11] This meant that the campaign would be waged in accordance with the French bombing plan and that the French air staff would have complete responsibility for nominating the targets. This arrangement was perfectly acceptable to the Admiralty, who were able to secure the use of a French base which was within operational range of the principal German industries. In any case, the French bombing plan was an eminently practical one and included many targets which the Navy wanted to attack.

This plan, which was issued in September 1916, was based on two main principles: first, that it was preferable to break down an industry at the source rather than attempt to destroy the many factories and workshops where the materials, for example steel or chemicals, were used; and secondly, that the tactical feasibility of operating against a particular target or group of targets should be the most important consideration in allocating a final order of priority. The basis of the plan was a list of objectives classified in decreasing importance according to their production of strictly war material. The first three on the list remained the same as in the original plan of 1915, only the order was different. Chemical works and explosive plants were still in first place, but iron foundries had replaced munition works in second place. Industries were also grouped geographically and the four most important centres, in order of priority, were as follows: (i) the Mannheim-Ludwigshafen group, (ii) the Main group, (iii) the Cologne group, (iv) Saar-Lorraine-Luxembourg group. The first three groups were, however, a great distance from the Allied lines, so the French placed the Saar-Lorraine-Luxembourg group at the head of the list, for the targets in this region fulfilled the vital condition of operational feasibility. All of them lay within a hundred kilometres of the main French base at Nancy and could therefore be subjected to frequent and systematic bombing. The next revision of the French bombing plan, approved on 12th March 1917, went one step further and limited the activity of the bombing aircraft to this region alone.[12]

Even if the question of operational feasibility is left out of account, this decision was a wise one. The region in which these three districts lay contained the richest deposits of iron ore in Europe, and the blast furnaces of the Saar, Lorraine, and Luxembourg produced roughly half of Germany's total output of steel. It was felt that if a considerable number of these furnaces could be put out of action Germany's output of munitions, which it was believed was barely sufficient for her needs, would be seriously reduced. Moreover, blast furnaces were conspicuous targets both by day and night and extremely vulnerable to attack. Not unnaturally, blast furnaces were the principal targets chosen by the French for the joint offensive, and most of these were situated in the Saar valley. This is hardly surprising since of the three areas only the Saar was German territory proper. Lorraine was part of that region of France – known to the French as Lorraine Annexée – which was absorbed by Germany in 1871, and Luxembourg had been occupied by German forces in 1914.

Shortly after the introduction of the French bombing plan in September 1916, the views expressed in it found support from an entirely independent quarter. A Belgian businessman whose work before the war had enabled him to gain an intimate knowledge of the European iron and steel industry wrote a letter to the Committee of Imperial Defence stressing the vulnerability of German steel production to air attack. His estimate was that fifty per cent of Germany's steel requirements were produced in Lorraine, Luxembourg and Alsace and that if the French and Belgian works in occupied territory were included the figure would be nearer seventy-five per cent. He was convinced that Germany was hard pressed to produce all the steel she needed to sustain her war effort; and to support this contention he stated that before the war a leading German steel manufacturer had told him that Germany realized that in the event of war her output of steel would not be sufficient unless she was able to secure the production of the Luxembourg and Lorraine areas.[13]

The War Trade Intelligence Department agreed with these estimates of Germany's reliance on steel produced outside Germany and supported the conclusion that the interruption of these supplies would be severely felt in Germany. Copies of the letter, together with favourable comments by the War Trade Intelligence Department and the War Office, were sent to the Admiralty and the French General Staff.[14] When the subject was raised at a meeting of the Air Board on 11th December 1916 Sir David Henderson made clear the attitude of the Flying Corps. 'He had not,' he stated, 'see the letter and did not think that the War Office were committed to an expression in favour of the policy involved.'[15] Among individual members of the Air Board there was certainly some interest shown in the proposals. Lord

Sydenham, who had previously been much in sympathy with Admiralty strategic policy, recorded his views in a minute dated 14th December 1916.

> Unless it can be distinctly shown that our armies on the Western front will be prejudiced, I am decidedly of the opinion that these steel works should be bombed to the fullest extent possible.[16]

But Lord Sydenham, like many others who were prepared to support a strategic air policy provided it did not interfere with the requirements of the armies on the Western Front, failed to appreciate that the demands for air resources in that theatre were insatiable.

* * *

As has been shown, the naval plans to attack German war industry had long been held in abeyance owing to the lack of a suitable bombing aircraft. However, the apprearance of the Sopwith 1½ Strutter in 1915 completely changed the situation, and enabled the Admiralty to put a definite proposal to the French for a joint offensive. The 1½ Strutter proved to be a most successful aeroplane and from the same type a bomber and fighter version were produced. The prototype of this aircraft was a two-seat biplane and this was the type used by the R.N.A.S. as a fighting machine. Known as the Admiralty type 9400, it was fitted with a Vickers gun for the pilot and a Lewis gun for the gunner. It had the same endurance as the bomber, about four hours, and could therefore escort the bomber formations all the way to the target. The bomber version, the Admiralty type 9700, was a single-seat aircraft which carried four 65 lb. bombs stowed internally. It is worthy of note that both versions of the naval Sopwith were the first British aircraft to be fitted with a really efficient synchronizing gear to enable the forward gun to fire through the arc of the airscrew.[17]

When it was apparent that deliveries of the Sopwith would be delayed longer than had been anticipated, the Admiralty purchased a number of French Breguet bombers in order to raise the strength of the wing to two squadrons. The type involved was a pusher biplane,[18] markedly inferior in performance to the Sopwith. Wing Commander R.B. Davies, V.C.[19] (later Vice-Admiral and author of *Sailor in the Air*) tested this aircraft and found that it was slower, carried less weight, and had a shorter range of action than the 1½ Strutter. Its main advantage was that it carried a gunner in the front cockpit and could therefore be defended from attack in all directions except below and astern.[20] The Breguet was not at all popular with the naval pilots who considered it was unsuitable for daylight operations which involved crossing the enemy lines.[21]

The comments of a Breguet pilot, Sub-Lieutenant H.E.P. Wigglesworth, who took part in the Oberndorf raid on 12th October, reflected the feelings of other pilots. In his report on the raid he suggested that 'Breguets could be far more safely used in night raids instead of during the day, at which time they require almost a fighter each'.[22] The French too had reached a similar conclusion and after the Oberndorf raid ruled that their pusher bombers – the Breguets and Farmans – were to be restricted to night operations.[23]

Among the most exacting duties on No. 3 Wing were those carried out by the Armament Officer whose chief responsibilities were for bombs, bomb-dropping gear and bombsights, all of which presented considerable technical difficulties. These difficulties were enhanced by the fact that the base in Lorraine lay a great distance from the nearest naval centres. There was no easy access to materials and equipment or to specialized skills, and in consequence the Wing had to rely largely on its own resources to tackle the problems created by the bombing operations. The officer who held this post during the greater part of No. 3 Wing's existence was Lieutenant Lord Tiverton, R.N.V.R.[24] whose outstanding work in planning strategic operations at the Air Ministry in 1918 will be described in a later chapter.

Though a barrister by profession, Lord Tiverton possessed a considerable knowledge of mathematics and scientific principles and this, together with an imaginative and enquiring mind, enabled him to undertake a detailed and systematic study of strategic bombing and the problems which it involved. He believed that strategic bombing could be made into a weapon of great striking power, but only if it were thoroughly understood. And this, he was convinced, could only be achieved by subjecting it to careful scientific scrutiny.

Beginning his work unofficially in 1915, he was able to pursue his investigations in an official capacity when he was appointed Armament Training Officer in the Air Department of the Admiralty, at the beginning of 1916. During the few months he held this post he concentrated his attention on ballistics and bomb-sighting. Characteristically, he completed a bomb-dropping course at Eastchurch to obtain the necessary practical experience. From the information on bomb-dropping which he gathered from the naval training stations, he quickly concluded that more data concerning the ballistics of various bombs were required before a more accurate sight could be constructed. To remedy this, he suggested that a number of bombs should be dropped from a tall chimney and their speeds of descent measured.[25] Experiments were in fact carried out by the Navy, in August and September 1916, to determine the 'fall' characteristics of certain bombs, but a mine shaft instead of a chimney was used.

When he was posted to No. 3 Wing in May 1916, Lord Tiverton was at once faced with the difficult problem of finding a suitable bombsight for the 1½ Strutter. Because of the poor view from the pilot's cockpit, both forward and below, neither of the two standard sights – the equal-distance and the C.F.S. – could be fitted. Again rating practical experience very highly, Lord Tiverton qualified as a pilot on a Curtiss J.N.4 and equipping one of these aircraft with a cockpit layout similar to that of the Sopwith

BE 2c's of No. 13 Squadron RFC at Gosport waiting to start for France, October 1915.
(*Photo: Imperial War Museum*)

Sopwith 1½ Strutter bombers of No. 3 Wing RNAS at Ochey 1917
(*Photo: R. C. B. Ashworth*)

Officers of No. 3 Wing RNAS:
Captain W. L. Elder and Wing Commander R. B. Davies V.C. (both seated) with
naval pilots, most of whom were Canadians.
(Photo: Canadian Forces Photo)

bomber he carried out experiments in the air to produce a practical bombsight. In the course of this work he designed various sights, but with only limited success.

One of the more successful sights consisted of a sighting hole cut in the floor of the aircraft to enable the pilot to keep the target in view. Across the sighting hole were fitted two transverse wires which were used in conjunction with a reversible stop watch to determine the instant of release. According to Vice-Admiral R.B. Davies, the chief drawback of this sight was that owing to the poor view from his cockpit the pilot had great difficulty in bringing the target into view through the sighting hole.[26] Trials were also carried out with a periscope type of sight, but this, too, proved difficult to operate.[27] On the other hand, the Breguets presented no problems; on these aircraft both the standard sights could be fitted and operated without undue trouble.

The summer of 1916 passed without any operations being undertaken in conjunction with the French force – the 4th Groupe de Bombardment. It was not until October, when the weather was already beginning to break, that a start could be made. By that time the strength of the naval force had just reached two squadrons: one squadron comprising two flights of 1½ Strutters, the other having one flight of 1½ Strutters and one flight of Breguets. Rather surprisingly, since the two forces had not operated together before and all but a few of the No. 3 Wing pilots lacked previous operational experience, the French chose a long-distance target – the Mauser factory at Oberndorf – for the first attack.[28]

This raid, involving a round flight of some 230 miles, was made in daylight on 12th October, the first day for some time that weather conditions over both the mountain areas to be crossed – the Vosges and Black Forest – were sufficiently favourable. Even so, the French commander did not receive a favourable weather report from his reconnaissance aircraft until early in the afternoon. The first flight took off at 1.15 p.m., the last one about an hour later – a schedule allowing only a narrow margin of time if

H

the aircraft were to complete the mission and return to base before nightfall. When the last naval flight (Sopwiths) took off at 2.15 p.m. conditions at base were beginning to deteriorate. A heavy layer of cloud had already formed, and because of this the aircraft of this flight failed to come together in formation. Following the strict instructions they had received, they returned to base without having crossed the lines.

Altogether thirty-four French and twenty-one British aircraft took part in the raid, and nine failed to return. Perhaps twenty actually bombed the target. Some, like the naval Breguets which Wing Commander Davies escorted in a Sopwith fighter, bombed another town which they mistook for Oberndorf.[29] On the face of it, not an unqualified success, but if account is taken of the fact that this difficult operation was the first Anglo-French effort, not by any means a failure, either. The unmistakable evidence which this raid offered was the extreme vulnerability of the French pushers in daylight, for of the nine allied aircraft, six French and three British, which failed to return, all but one were Breguets and Farmans. The French drew the inevitable conclusion from those casualties and restricted their bombing to night operations. It is seldom worthwhile to speculate as to what might have happened in different circumstances, but in this case it is hard to resist the temptation to ask what the result would have been if the majority of the aircraft had been Sopwiths. It seems almost certain that greater damage would have been inflicted on the enemy for a fraction of the loss.

The German military authorities were well satisfied with the outcome of their first clash with the allied bombers. It was something they had no desire to hide from the German public, so they released to the press a full account of the raid. In particular, they spared no detail concerning the destruction of the nine allied aircraft of which, it was stated, eight were accounted for by fighters and one by the ground defences. The *Frankfurter Zeitung* was able to quote the types of the destroyed aircraft, including in some cases the aircraft squadron numbers, and to indicate the place where each one was brought down.[30] Such an account however contained the obvious admission that a considerable force of British and French bombers had penetrated deep into German territory. And an intelligent German reader might have drawn a conclusion similar to that which Captain R.M. Groves R.N., assistant secretary of the Air Board, had reached after reading the Allied reports: that 'the fighting took place well back in German territory, clearly showing that the Germans have deflected a strong fighting force to deal with the menace of long range bombing'.[31]

The tactics employed by the naval squadrons were simple but effective. The operational unit on a bombing mission was the flight which consisted of five or six aircraft. The flights took off at approximately ten minute intervals, and having come together in a V formation, set course for the target in company with their fighter escorts. Great importance was attached to close formation flying which provided the most effective defence against hostile aircraft, and pilots received strict orders to return to base if they failed to pick up formation with the other aircraft in their flight.[32] The flights found their way to the target by map-reading and in daylight this was a satisfactory method of navigation since there were many easily identifiable objects in the area in which the wing operated. On reaching the vicinity of the target, the flight formed into a line and each aircraft bombed in succession. When all the aircraft had dropped their bombs, the flight again assumed formation and set course for base.[33]

After the Oberndorf raid, the French turned their attention to the targets which headed the list on their bombing plan, namely, the blast furnaces and steel works. Since most of these plants lay well to the north of Luxeuil, the French issued instructions to the naval squadrons to move their base of operations, first, to Nancy, and shortly afterwards, to Ochey, twelve miles south-west of Nancy, in order to shorten the distances to the intended objectives. The first naval Sopwiths to move to the Nancy area did so at a few hours' notice on 22nd October, the object being to make preparations for a raid in conjunction with the French 4th

Groupe de Bombardment. The target was the Thyssen iron works at Hagendingen which the French attacked on the night of 22nd October.[34] On the following day, the British carried out a daylight raid on the same target and this proved to be most successful. Admiral Davies described the raid in his book *Sailor in the Air*.

> During our share of it there was heavy but inaccurate AA fire near the front, but we saw no German aircraft. The French attacks during the night had obviously done serious damage to the furnaces which appeared to be cold when we arrived. Our aircraft kept excellent formation, moved into single line and went down to bomb in succession, and I could see the bombs bursting amongst the furnace buildings. The return journey was uneventful, with little AA fire.[35]

After the Hagendingen raid, weather conditions began to deteriorate and heavy fogs in the river valleys in which the main objectives were situated added to the difficulties. Nevertheless, four raids were made in November: two against the steel works at Volklingen, and one each against the blast furnaces at St. Ingbert and Dillingen. But in December only one attack — against the blast furnaces at Dillingen — was possible. By the end of the year the operational efficiency of the naval wing had reached a high standard, and the Sopwith pilots were confident of their ability not only to locate and bomb their targets but also to deal with any enemy aircraft which attempted to interfere with them.

> When we went to attack [recorded Admiral Davies] we usually met with the same half-hearted interference from German aircraft and the self-confidence of our young pilots rose rapidly. My idea was to keep the flights in close-locked formation, with fighters supporting the bombers on the outward and return journeys. However the bomber pilots had discovered that once their bomb loads were gone they had the legs of the fighters. So as soon as their bombs had been

Area of Operations
of No. 3 Wing R.N.A.S.
and the 41st Wing and
the Independent Force

released, they took to opening throttle and going off on their
own in search of Germans. I gave up trying to stop this as it
was resulting in quite a number of Germans shot down.[36]

From the beginning, the Allied raids caused serious concern to
the Germans who possessed only a rudimentary air defence
system. It is true that French bombing attacks against Germany in
the summer of 1916 had compelled the German military
authorities to give attention to the question of air defence, and by
the early autumn units of single-seat fighters had been deployed in
the industrial areas of western Germany from Cologne to Freiburg.
But these were too few in number to deal effectively with the
systematic bombing which was being developed by the Allies. In
any case there was almost no co-ordination between these flying
units and such ground defences as existed. The Germans made the
first move to change this situation in October 1916 when a home
air defence command was created. Arrangements were at once put
in hand to provide more guns and searchlights for an organized
defence of important industrial centres.[37] In addition, the fighter
defence force was strengthened, and evidence of this was provided
by Captain Elder when he visited the Air Board in London on
25th October. In an unofficial report which was circulated among
the members of the Board, he stated that:

> . . . one result of their presence at Luxeuil had been to cause
> the Germans to establish very large aerial forces, opposite to
> them both immediately behind the lines and also further
> back, which forces must presumably have been deflected
> from service at the front.

Captain Elder also stated that 'four German aerodromes had
been established since their arrival and there were many more
being fitted out'.[38] The Allied bombing also caused demands from
many German factories for protection in the form of balloon and
kite barrages.

Barrage detachments [stated the Official Historian] were allocated to the Saar, to the Lorraine-Luxembourg, and to the Rhineland industrial areas. Although they were said to have entailed an excessive expenditure of time, labour, and equipment, and were, in consequence, disliked by the German military authorities, the effect on the moral of the workers was reckoned to be so great thatadditional barrage detachments were subsequently formed.[39]

In spite of the enemy's efforts to strengthen his defences the naval squadrons continued to bomb their objectives by day without undue hindrance from anti-aircraft guns or fighters. The reason for this immunity was that the German resources in guns and aircraft were just not sufficient to provide even the most elementary defence for the vulnerable areas. Even the single-seat fighter units which might have proved a formidable obstacle to the bombers were too scattered to be effective. Wing Commander Davies pointed to the difficulties facing the Germans in a report dated 4th January 1917.[40]

Up to the present, German machines have in nearly all cases avoided engaging machines in the V and have waited to attack stragglers. They have on more than one occasion been seen flying high above the flight and have not come down to attack, though on these occasions they have been greatly inferior in numbers. Beyond sending up a few fast fighters to look for a chance of attacking stragglers, it does not appear that the Germans have yet made any counter organization to deal with raids in this neighbourhood. The difficulty in their way is principally the number of machines with which they have to deal. It is easy to keep a small number of machines constantly on patrol duty, or to keep a small number constantly ready to go up, but small numbers can do little more than attack stragglers.

Wing Commander Davies was however convinced that the immunity then enjoyed by the naval aircraft would not continue indefinitely. It was therefore necesssary to consider whether new bombing tactics would be needed to counteract likely improvements in the German fighter defence system. He thought it would be a great advantage if the escort fighters had more powerful engines and possessed a better general performance than the bombers they were protecting. The German patrols would, he wrote, 'be greatly embarrassed if we possessed a flight of fast single seater fighters, such as Sopwith Pups or Triplanes, which could climb to the height of the German machines'.

But this was only touching the surface of the problem. What had to be decided was whether the present system of using single-seat bombers with their escorts of two-seater fighters would continue to be effective. Wing Commander Davies doubted whether this would be so, especially if the Germans extended their use of two-seater fighters. He thought that if the enemy operated these aeroplanes in groups of sufficient size to outnumber the escort fighters, the bombers would have to break formation to engage them.

In the event of the Germans organizing flights of this description to defeat raids, it is probable that the single seater bomber will not prove the ideal machine. It will be of great importance for the bombers to defend themselves without breaking formation. The type most suitable for this will be a two-seater bomber, but it will not be an advantage if speed, climb or manoeuvring power have to be sacrificed to obtain the extra lift required. In my opinion it will be well worth experimenting with a type of machine similar to the present Sopwith, but carrying a passenger and gun and a greatly reduced weight of bombs. With such machines there will be no need of escorting fighters, and all machines in the flight will then not be very greatly reduced, while it is probable that very greatly increased accuracy of dropping will be obtained by carrying a passenger to work the sighting arrangements.

The last consideration Wing Commander Davies held to be of the greatest importance, for he emphasized the fact that all pilots experienced difficulty in operating a bombsight while flying an aircraft. Further, when several aircraft were attacking a target in rapid succession, the pilots had almost no way of determining the accuracy of their bomb-aiming, since they could seldom see where their bombs burst.

Clearly Wing Commander Davies believed that the ascendancy then enjoyed by the day bombers would be brought to an end as soon as the Germans came to grips with the problems of air defence. He had therefore expressed his ideas on how bombing tactics should be modified to meet the inevitable improvement in the enemy fighter defence. These ideas, the basis of which was a bomber force composed of two-seater aircraft, were shared by Captain Elder who in an earlier paper described in greater detail what he believed would be the characteristics of the day bomber of the future.

The ideal machine for bombing would be a comparatively small machine (such as the 1½ Strutter) but capable of carrying a passenger for defence purposes, speed as fast as possible, and good climb with fuel for a range in still air of 600 to 650 miles.

He thought that it would carry two or more 65 lb. bombs, but in no circumstances should the bomb load be increased to the detriment of the aircraft's speed.[41]

In the early months of 1917 the weather cleared considerably, but the cloudless skies brought low temperatures. In February especially, the cold was so intense that in the unheated hangars of Ochey the oil in the aircraft engines froze, and though blowlamps and heaters were used, only a small number of machines could be kept in flying condition.[42] In January and February, bombing operations were restricted to two missions — one in each month — against the blast furnaces at Burbach.[43] At the end of February the weather became milder, but even when conditions were in other respects suitable for operational flying, thick fogs frequently covered the areas in which the important industrial targets were situated. In March the operational record improved: the blast furnaces at Burbach were attacked twice, and a raid was made on the aerodrome at Morhange.[44]

By early 1917 arrangements had been made to add a night bomber squadron to the naval force. The aircraft with which the squadron was to be equipped was the Handley Page 0/100. This was a new aircraft produced to an Admiralty specification, of December 1914, for a two-seater machine, with a speed of not less than 75 m.p.h. and capable of carrying a minimum of six 112 lb. bombs. The prototype of the 0/100 made its maiden flight in December 1915, and the first service aircraft was delivered to No. 3 Wing in November 1916.[45] The first operation of this new bomber was a raid carried out by a single aircraft on the night of 16-17th March against the railway station at Moulin-les-Metz.[46]

After the raid, Squadron Commander J.T. Babington, the officer commanding the squadron, submitted an operational report to Captain Elder. In it he stated that the Handley Page had had no difficulty 'in lifting 12 (100 lb.) bombs and 5½ hours fuel' and expressed his opinion that it would prove to be 'entirely satisfactory and reliable' as a night bomber.[47] Unfortunately the plans to equip a full squadron did not mature, and when orders to disband the naval force were received on 25th March 1917 the squadron possessed only two aircraft. Nevertheless, the night bombers continued to operate after normal daylight missions had ceased, and during the month of April single Handley Pages carried out attacks against the railway junction at Arnaville, the blast furnaces at Hagendingen and the depot and aerodrome at Chambley.[48]

The orders to disband the wing were contained in an Admiralty

signal of 25th March. This was followed shortly afterwards by a
letter giving detailed instructions for the closing down. Then a
second signal, dated 1st April, postponed the disbandment to
allow a reprisal raid to be carried out against a German city.[49] The
target chosen was Freiburg in Breisgau and the reason for the raid
was the torpedoing of two hospital ships – *Asturias* and
Gloucester Castle – during the latter half of March. Without
hesitation, the French agreed to take part, and on 14th April
twenty-five British and fifteen French aircraft made two attacks
on Freiburg. There is no doubt that the raid was a true reprisal, for
the reports of the British pilots make clear that their aiming point
was the centre of the town.[50]

In spite of its short duration the bombing campaign of the naval
wing was remarkably successful, and this can in part be explained
by the advantages enjoyed by the Allies in this type of warfare. A
large number of the industries vital to the German war effort lay
in western Germany, near to the frontier, in Luxembourg, and in
Alsace and Lorraine, the two annexed French provinces, and were
therefore within range of the allied aerodromes in France. And the
distribution of war industries within these areas favoured the
Allies. Broadly speaking, they were contained within a fairly
narrow band, running roughly north and south, and extending
over something like two hundred miles. The task of providing
adequate defences against air attack on so wide a front was quite
beyond the resources of the Germans. The most they could do was
to position such guns, searchlights and aeroplanes as could be
diverted from the front in and around the most vulnerable areas.
Nevertheless, the Germans had taken warning from the French
bombing raids of 1916 and by the spring of the following year had
established an elementary defence system. Even so, this would not
have been sufficient to ward off attacks on the scale which the
French and British could well have achieved by the summer of
1917.

The effect produced on Germany by the brief Anglo-French
offensive is well summed up by the Official Historian who had

somewhat modified his views concerning this episode when the last volume was written in the mid 1930's.

> With our fuller knowledge it is clear that the effect produced by the naval bombing wing was disproportionate to the number of raids, which were comparatively infrequent and are not to be judged by the material results. The British and French bombing attacks went some way to shake the morale of the industrial population and had an adverse effect on the output of munitions of war, but chiefly they compelled the Germans to divert aeroplanes, labour, and material to the beginnings of widespread schemes of home defence.[51]

Soon after the disbandment of No. 3 Wing, the Dunkirk Wing began to re-equip with two new aircraft, the Handley Page 0/100 and the D.H.4 which transformed the striking power of the force. Though the Handley Page had established itself as a night bomber with No. 3 Wing, it was initially used as a day bomber when it came into service at Dunkirk in April 1917. But as a result of the experience gained from these early operations, it was decided to restrict its activities to night raids. At first, the night attacks were carried out only during moonlight conditions, but as the crews became more experienced in night flying, operations were attempted on any night when weather conditions were generally good.[52] Indeed the success of these operations convinced the Navy that there were many advantages inherent in night bombing, and a report which the Dunkirk commander prepared for the Air Board was mainly responsible for persuading that body of the importance of night operations in long-range air warfare.[53]

The advantages of night bombing carried out by well-trained and experienced crews were in fact obvious. Owing to the almost complete absence of effective anti-aircraft defences during the hours of darkness, the night bomber could be designed almost exclusively as a weight carrier. It did not need to be a fast or well-defended aircraft and could bomb from low altitudes because anti-aircraft gunfire was little to be feared at night.[54] In addition, the difficulties inherent in flying in the dark were partly overcome because the night bomber could carry a sufficiently large crew to enable each member to perform a specialized function. For instance, the observer, who dropped the bombs, moved from his seat beside the pilot into the front cockpit during the run-up to the target. There he operated the bombsight which was fixed on the nose of the aircraft. Further, in an aircraft of this size there was, relatively speaking, sufficient room and comfort for the crew to employ navigational methods similar to those used by ships at sea. In fact, the instruments which the Navy was then beginning to produce in order to reduce the element of guesswork in air navigation were at first mainly used in the night bombers.

The D.H.4 day bomber, which also came into service with the R.N.A.S. in the spring of 1917,[55] closely resembled the type of aircraft envisaged by Captain Elder and Wing Commander Davies to replace the single-seat Sopwith 1½ Strutter. The new bomber was a two-seater aircraft, and the observer-gunner who occupied the rear cockpit could if necessary operate the bombsight. Powered by a 250 horse-power Rolls-Royce engine, it had a maximum speed of 115 m.p.h. and could climb fully loaded to 16,000 feet. Nor was this extra performance gained at the expense of the aircraft's weight-carrying capacity, for the D.H.4 carried as a normal load four 112 lb. bombs. By virtue of its speed, rate of climb, and ceiling, the D.H.4 was a match for most enemy fighters, and when flying in properly organized formations was capable of providing its own defence against hostile aircraft.

The rearming of the naval squadrons with these new aircraft should have enabled the Dunkirk force to intensify its long-range bombing campaign during the summer of 1917. Unfortunately, however, the growing power of the force was largely neutralized by an extension of the range of targets it was required to attack. Clearly, its principal objectives should have been the German naval bases along the Belgian coast; but to these were added the aerodromes in Belgium from which German bombers were operating against England and the wide variety of targets nominated by the Army in connection with the land campaign. Indeed, this was not a new situation. Ever since the Dunkirk force had been formed, early in the war, it had been given too many diverse tasks to allow a sufficient concentration of strength for strategic bombing. This weakness was to a great extent brought about by the willingness of the Vice-Admiral of the Dover Patrol to place his squadrons under the C-in-C of the B.E.F. whenever he could reasonably do so. As has been shown, Admiral Bacon was convinced that air power, to be effective, had to be exercised in sub-ordination to naval or military operations. If therefore his squadrons were not required in direct support of naval operations, he had no objection to their being used in conjunction with the military campaign. He refused to accept the belief, which sustained the policy of the Air Department of the Admiralty, that independent bombing operations, if pursued systematically and in sufficient strength, could by themselves exert an important influence on the outcome of the war.

The views of Admiral Bacon were not shared by Captain Lambe, commander of the Dunkirk squadrons, and this fact was made very clear in a report which he sent to the Admiral for transmission to the Admiralty in February 1918. In this report he repeated what he had previously recorded in official papers: that the value of bombing, provided it was carried out contin-uously and by large numbers of aircraft, could hardly be overestimated. He was convinced that if heavy air attacks were made against enemy naval targets the output of the naval bases, submarine building yards, and factories would be 'very materially decreased'. But in the case of objectives at short-range he went further and stated his belief that if a sufficient number of aircraft were available for both day and night attacks an important base such as Bruges harbour could be rendered untenable.

This statement [he continued] may appear sweeping, but I am convinced of its truth, and if the question be raised as to why the activity of submarines operating from Bruges has been so little affected in the past, it must be pointed out that the few machines which were available have been utilized largely in connection with Military Operations, and the sphere of operations extended over the whole area of the North of Belgium, bounded by the line Thorout-Ghent-Brussels-Antwerp, with occasional attacks on very distant objectives; hence it has never been possible to concentrate on any one objective, machines available being utilized to fulfil the Military requirements of the moment.[56]

When however Captain Lambe stated these views the opportunity for the Dunkirk force to make a contribution to the strategic air war had virtually ended. For political reasons, the British Government had already decreed the formation of a long-range bomber force in the Nancy area to carry out raids into Germany in retaliation for German aircraft attacks against London. And since there were no 'spare' squadrons to send to Nancy, the nucleus of the new force was created by withdrawing units from the Dunkirk force and from the military squadrons of the B.E.F. Thereafter, the position in respect of the supply of aircraft improved only slowly, and during 1918 the expansion of the force at Nancy retarded the growth of the Dunkirk squadrons. Though the force continued to operate as No. 5 Group R.A.F. after the amalgamation of the two air services, its activities until the end of the war were overshadowed by the bombing operations of the Independent Force.

By the spring of 1917 the leaders of the Flying Corps had achieved all their aims in their dispute with the Admiralty. They had caused the bombing wing at Luxeuil to be disbanded and had secured from the Navy four fully equipped fighting squadrons and a large number of aero-engines. Moreover, they were certain of the support of the Dunkirk bombing squadrons during the proposed summer offensive. Strategic operations were now virtually at an end, and almost the whole of British air power in the western theatre was committed to the support of land operations on the Western Front.

Yet to judge from the subsequent air battles of 1917 the German air force does not seem to have been unduly embarrassed by the extra strength brought against it. Indeed, the account of the battle of Arras contained in the Official History lends support to the view that the Germans had the better of the air fighting during this period.[57] On the other hand it can hardly be doubted that the removal of No. 3 Wing brought great relief to the Germans to whom the provision of an air defence system (no matter how inadequate) was an intolerate burden. Most of the material and personnel employed on home defence were obtained at the expense of the armies at the front and this is shown by the fact that during the battle of Arras the Germans were able to send air re-inforcements to the Arras sector soon after the disbandment of No. 3 Wing.[58]

Nevertheless, the naval wing had, during its brief life, influenced the air war in a way that has often been overlooked. It created a situation in which for the first time since 1914 the initiative in the strategic air war passed to the British. Since early 1915 German airships had carried out sporadic raids against Britain.[59] These were, in the main, light, and scattered and caused little material damage, but the injury which they inflicted upon Britain's war effort was considerable. Their most serious effect was on war production, for the report of even a single raider would cause factories to stop work over a large area. In addition, the raids did much to depress the morale of the civil population and led to continual public demands for greater anti-aircraft protection. As a military weapon the Zeppelin was largely ineffective, yet the Government was unable to resist public pressure to devote an ever increasing amount of equipment and number of personnel to home defence. By the end of 1916 there were over 17,000 officers and men retained in Great Britain specifically for this purpose. Nor was the R.F.C. contribution an inconsiderable one, and amounted to 200 officers, 2,000 men and 110 aeroplanes.[60]

Sopwith 1½ Strutter of No. 3 Wing showing open bomb doors.
(*Photo: Imperial War Museum*)

Breguet V of the RNAS 1917. Note the equal-distance bombsight.
(*Photo: J. M. Bruce: G. S. Leslie Collection*).

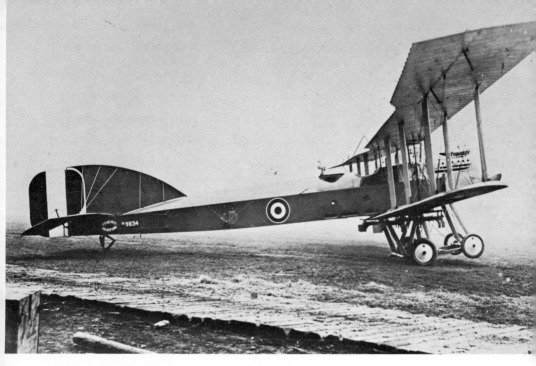

Short bomber of the RNAS, 1916
(*Photo: J. M. Bruce: G. S. Leslie Collection*).

FE 2b night bomber of No. 100 Squadron, RFC, Western Front 1917.
(*Photo: Imperial War Museum*).

The operations of No. 3 Wing had created, for the first time, similar problems for the Germans. Demands from the civil population for better protection against air raids compelled the German government to build up a defence system at great cost both in men and material. But in one important respect the German position was worse. Whereas the Zeppelins were seldom able to locate and bomb their objectives at night,[61] the naval bombers, operating in more favourable conditions and at a shorter range, had proved themselves capable of finding and bombing specific targers both by day and night. In consequence, these operations were far more dangerous to the Germans than the airship raids had ever been to the British. When therefore the operations of the naval wing were brought to an end, the Germans were not merely relieved of serious pressure on their western frontier, but, as will be shown, were allowed to regain the initiative in the strategic air war.

I

Chapter 5

The New Strategic Air Policy and the Creation of the Royal Air Force, June 1917 – March 1918

As early as the autumn of 1914 the Germans had made plans to use aeroplanes in bombing attacks against England. A bomber squadron was formed at Ostend, but when Calais, the base from which the aircraft were intended to operate, did not fall into German hands the plans were abandoned, for the aircraft of that period did not possess the capability of operating from more distant bases.[1] Instead, attacks against Britain were made at long range by airships based on the north German coast. It was not until the end of 1916, when the weaknesses of the Zeppelin were all too apparent, that the Germans were able to revive the aeroplane plan. The reason for this was the production of a new bomber, the Gotha (type G.IV), a twin-engined aircraft whose performance opened up new possibilities in the air war against England. In the autumn of 1916, General von Hoeppner, Commander of the German military air service, gave orders for a squadron of these aircraft to be formed so that London, now a target of great difficulty for airships, would again feel the weight of German bombs.[2]

Early in 1917 the aircraft and personnel began to assemble at the Belgian aerodromes of St. Denis Westrem and Gontrode, but because of the lengthy preparations required to bring the squadron up to the required standard of efficiency, it was not until the last week in May that the first raid against England was made.[3]

On the 25th of that month, twenty-one Gothas crossed the Essex coast at about 5 p.m., heading for London, but heavy cloud over Essex caused them to turn south over Kent and attack Shorncliffe and Folkstone instead. Neither of these towns had been notified of the approach of hostile aircraft, and because of this failure casualties were high, amounting to 95 killed and 195 injured. Many naval and military aircraft took off to intercept the raiders, but few of them were capable of reaching the height at which the Gothas were operating. As the bombers crossed the Channel on the return flight, they were engaged by fighters from Dunkirk and one was destroyed and another damaged. This first daylight attack revealed serious deficiencies in the air defences. The communications system for reporting the movements of enemy aircraft had broken down, and the aircraft used on home defence duties were not sufficiently up-to-date to deal with the new German bombers. In any case, a system which relied upon a number of individual aircraft searching for the raiders was bound to be ineffective. Even if a single aircraft did succeed in attacking the enemy squadron, it would be outgunned by the bombers flying in formation.[4]

This was only the beginning. After an attack on Shoeburyness and Sheerness on 5th June, the German bombers made their first daylight raid on London on 13th June. Fourteen Gothas reached their objective just after 11.30 a.m. and dropped their bombs on the east part of the city, their main aiming point being the area around Liverpool Street Station. The total casualties, 162 killed and 432 injured, were the highest of any one raid on this country during the war. It was recorded that 92 aircraft of all types took off to intercept the raiders, but scarcely any of them obtained even a glimpse of the enemy aircraft, all of which returned safely to their bases.[5]

The Government were thoroughly alarmed by this unexpected development in the air war, and on the day following the raid the Cabinet decided that there should be a substantial increase in the air services. During the following two weeks various schemes were drafted and discussed, and on 2nd July the Cabinet approved a plan to increase the strength of the R.F.C. from 108 to 200 service squadrons, with a corresponding increase in the strength of the R.N.A.S. Already the Cabinet had considered the feasibility of making a retaliatory raid against a city in Germany, such as Mannheim, and had examined a proposal to withdraw fighting squadrons from the Western Front to strengthen home defences.[6]

A few days after the raid on London Sir Douglas Haig came to England to discuss with the Government his proposed offensive in Flanders. On this visit he was accompanied by General Trenchard whose views on air defence the Cabinet were anxious to hear at first hand. At a cabinet meeting on 20th June Trenchard stated that in his opinion the most effective way to defeat the air attacks would be for the Allies to gain possession of the Belgian coast.[7] If this could be achieved, the enemy bombers would have to fly over territory controlled by the Allies both on the outward and return flights, thus making their operations extremely hazardous. The next most effective course of action would be to intensify attacks upon German air units behind the Western Front in order to reduce the enemy's capacity to operate against Britain. Such attacks, he said, were being carried out but were limited by the resources available. On the question of air patrols, he thought that any system of patrols, to be effective, would require far greater numbers of aircraft and pilots than could be provided, but conceded that temporary patrols operating on both sides of the Channel could be established.[8]

After hearing these views, the Cabinet decided that temporary patrols should be operated and, accordingly, issued the necessary instructions to Haig who moved No. 56 Squadron to Canterbury and No. 66 Squadron to Calais. The two squadrons remained on watch for two weeks and were then ordered back to their bases. Almost immediately afterwards, the Gothas appeared over London in daylight for the second time.[9] This was on the morning of Saturday 7th July, when twenty-one bombers, having approached from the north, dropped their bombs on the City and East End. The total casualties were 54 killed and 190 injured. Again, the impotence of the defence forces was shown, for although 95 naval and military aircraft took off in pursuit, only one Gotha was destroyed.[10]

The news of the second raid on London came as a great shock to the public. People found it incredible that enemy aeroplanes should be able to fly with impunity over England in daylight. Hitherto, opinion in the country had shown great understanding of the difficulties of combating night raiders, but this under-standing did not extend to the failure to prevent the daylight attacks on London. Now, those responsible for home defence (the military authorities since early 1916) bore the full force of public indignation, an intensity of feeling only surpassed by the anger directed against the Germans for what was considered to be their barbaric attacks upon civilians.

Few would have dared openly to disagree with this condem-nation of the German action, whatever their private feelings. One who had the courage to do so was Lord Montagu. Soon after the first raid, he stated in the House of Lords that since London was an important centre for the production of war materials it was a perfectly legitimate target for attack. This statement was greeted with a storm of protest (much of it hysterical), and Lord Montagu was accused of justifying the killing of civilians. Typical of this was the attack upon what was called the Montague Doctrine in the editorial column of the periodical *Flying*.

> Lord Montagu exonerates the Germans. He grants them full absolution. He gives them carte blanche. He hands them a blank cheque. The Montagu Doctrine covers any and every form of indiscriminate bomb-dropping. There is no limit whatever to the slaughter of civilians that may be lawfully carried out by squadrons of aircraft flying at a height which precludes the possibility of aiming at a military objective. Apparently, the Montagu Doctrine would justify the extermi-nation of every man, woman and child in London; for if it be justifiable to slay a hundred civilians it would be justifiable to slay a million or five millions.[11]

Writing in the next issue of the same journal, F.W. Lanchester, a member of the Advisory Committee for Aeronautics, expressed a saner view of the raid and its effect on the public.

> That London should have been subjected to a second raid in force by an enemy squadron cannot have given rise to the least surprise or astonishment. Such an event was expected sooner or later for long enough before the first raid took place on June 13th, and since that date a repetition has been looked upon as little less than a certainty. What has astonished London and caused widespread indignation is the fact that the attacking squadron apparently found its way over with as little interference as though it had been executing a spectacular manoeuvre at a parade or review in its country of origin.[12]

Within a few hours of the raid a Cabinet meeting was held to discuss possible means of bringing the attacks to an end. After a somewhat confused session, the Cabinet resolved that two fighting squadrons should be withdrawn from the B.E.F. for defence duties at home and that, if possible, a raid should be carried out against Mannheim. Sir Douglas Haig was instructed to give effect to these decisions and he at once made arrangements for the two squadrons to be despatched. However, in a telegram notifying the Government of his action, Haig issued a warning that if both the orders were carried out the impending military operations in France would be placed in jeopardy. This communication caused the Government to reconsider its decision and to rule that only one squadron need be sent from France and that the Mannheim raid should be postponed until suitable bombing aircraft were available.[13]

Up to that time government action had consisted of temporary measures designed to ensure that if the German bombers returned to London they would meet with stiffer opposition than before. The wider problem of creating an efficient defence system still remained to be dealt with, and in this connection the Government was determined that any examination of Britain's defence arrangements would form part of a review of the nation's air policy and organization as a whole. Accordingly, at a cabinet meeting on 11th July, the decision was taken to set up a committee to examine, first, the defence arrangements for home defence against air raids, and secondly, the air organization generally and the higher direction of aerial operations. Lloyd George, the Prime Minister, appointed a two-man committee of which he himself was the chairman. But all the work was done by Lieutenant-General J.C. Smuts, the South African soldier and statesman, who was a member of the War Cabinet.

General Smuts set to work at once and accomplished his task with remarkable speed and thoroughness. He first tackled the problems of air defence and submitted his report to the Cabinet on 19th July. He then investigated the fields of air policy and organization, and the recommendations contained in his second report, dated 17th August 1917, led to the creation of an independent air service and to the formation of an air policy which was to be the basis of all R.A.F. thought for the following twenty-five years.[14]

In the first part of his report General Smuts stated his conviction that there was no justification for continuing to subordinate the air services to the needs of the Navy and the Army. He compared the air arm with a branch like the artillery which could only be used as an ancillary to naval or military operations.

Air Service on the contrary can be used as an independent means of war operations. Nobody that witnessed the attack on London on 11th (sic) July could have any doubt on that point.

General Smuts himself had been in London during the raid on 7th July, and the sight of the German aircraft striking directly at London from distant bases convinced him of the immense potential of strategic bombing. He was also deeply impressed by what he had seen of the effect of the bombing on the morale of the civilian population.[1][5]

> And the day may not be far off, [he predicted] when aerial operations with their devastation of enemy lands and destruction of industrial and populous centres on a vast scale may become the principal operations of war, to which the older forms of military and naval operations may become secondary and subordinate.

But if Britain was to secure the advantages which would accrue from such operations, steps must be taken to ensure an adequate supply of suitable aircraft and to provide for the effective direction of air strategy. Neither of these, General Smuts believed, would be unduly difficult to achieve.

> The programme of aircraft production which the War Cabinet has sanctioned for the following twelve months is far in excess of Navy and Army requirements. Next spring and summer the position will be that the Army and Navy will have all the Air Service required in connection with their operations; and over and above that there will be a great surplus available for independent operations. Who is to look after and direct the activities of this available surplus? Neither the Army nor the Navy is specially competent to do so; and for that reason the creation of an Air Staff for planning and directing independent air operations will soon be pressing.

General Smuts acknowledged that it was no easy matter to grasp the immensity of the change in warfare which he was suggesting might be brought about by strategic bombing.

> It requires some imagination to realize that next summer,

while our Western Front may still be moving forward at a snail's pace in Belgium and France, the air battle-front will be far behind on the Rhine, and that its continuous and intense pressure against the chief industrial centres of the enemy as well as on his lines of communication may form an important factor in bringing about peace.

He had no doubt that the enemy was already making plans for an onslaught on London and that the only way of wrecking that scheme was to defeat him in the air and carry 'the war into the heart of his country'.

The importance which the long-range bomber would shortly attain was, General Smuts believed, a manifestation of the changing nature of the war. It was now no longer manpower but arms and machines which would exert the decisive influence on the outcome of the struggle, and the side that achieved superiority in industrial production, and exploited that advantage to the full, would almost certainly win the war.

The submarine has already shown [he stated] what startling developments are possible in naval warfare. Aircraft is destined to work an even more far-reaching change in land warfare. But to secure the advantages of this new factor for our side we must not only make unlimited use of the mechanical genius and productive capacity of ourselves and our American allies, we must create the new directing organization, the new Ministry and Air Staff which could properly handle this new instrument of offensive, and equip it with the best brains at our disposal for the purpose. The task of planning the new Air Service organization and thinking out and preparing for schemes of aerial operations next summer must tax our air experts to the utmost and no time should be lost in setting the new Ministry and staff going.

In the main official opinion was favourably disposed to the idea of creating a force of bombing aircraft to launch against Germany. It was however far from being convinced that this desirable scheme could be put into practice. In particular, doubts were cast upon the validity of the two assumptions — one explicit, the other implicit — on which the recommendations were based. These were, first, that there would be a large surplus of aircraft by the summer of 1918, and secondly, that it would be possible to set up a new ministry during the stresses of war without seriously disrupting the air services. In view of the vital nature of these assumptions in relation to the report, it will be instructive to discover how General Smuts came to accept them.

As has been shown, the two basic recommendations of the report were that a long-range bomber force should be created to strike directly at the heart of Germany, and that a new ministry should be set up to formulate and direct the policy governing the employment of the bomber force. Both these recommendations, however, depended upon the availability of a surplus of aircraft from which, it is clear, General Smuts intended the bomber force should be created. For it is absolutely certain that General Smuts would not have advised the Government to undertake a major reorganization of the air services in wartime if he had not been convinced that strategic air power could be used to influence the outcome of the war.

All then depended upon the ability of British industry to produce a large number of aircraft in excess of the requirements already foreseen. General Smuts was led to believe that this could be achieved by no less a person than Lord Cowdray, president of the second Air Board. It seems that Lord Cowdray, who worked with great energy to improve the output of aircraft, was convinced that his efforts were soon to produce results. His reading of the situation was that the production of aircraft for 1918 would greatly exceed expectations, and that in consequence there would be a surplus of aircraft after the requirements of the Navy and the Army had been met. It was his opinion that these surplus aeroplanes (the 'Surplus Aircraft Fleet' was his term) should be used to create a bomber force.[16]

When General Smuts was informed by Lord Cowdray that a surplus of aircraft would be available in 1918 he based his inquiry on the assumption that the information was accurate. In the event, Lord Cowdray's estimates proved to be wide of the mark, but General Smuts did not discover this until some time after his report was completed.

Haig and Trenchard were immediately suspicious of promises of improved supplies of aircraft.

> After more than three years of war, [wrote Haig after studying the report] our armies are still very far short of their requirements, and my experience of repeated failures to fulfil promises as regards provision makes me somewhat sceptical as to the large surplus of machines and personnel on which the Committee counts. ... Moreover that surplus is calculated on a statement of requirements rendered fifteen months ago, to which additions had to be made in November last and to which still further additions may have to be made. Nor is it clear that the large provision necessary to replace wastage has been sufficiently taken into account.[17]

By the time Smuts received Haig's communication he was already beginning to suspect that he had been misled by Cowdray's estimates, and this impression was strengthened when he discussed the matter with Trenchard in London early in October.[18]

The question of the establishment in wartime of a new ministry remains to be considered. It is obvious that General Smuts had the support of someone with the necessary experience in administration and in air matters to undertake the task of reorganization. And that person was Sir David Henderson. Indeed it could hardly have been anyone else, for of the handful of Flying Corps officers who possessed the necessary rank to undertake such a task, none had sufficient personal authority or experience of administration at that level.

From the very beginning, Henderson had made his position clear. In a memorandum to Smuts, he stated that the task would be difficult, but not impossible, and suggested that if it was anticipated that the war would not end before June 1918, it should certainly be undertaken.[19] It seems that Smuts was greatly impressed by Henderson's grasp of the situation and constantly sought his advice during the period when the report on air policy and organization was being prepared.[20] Without doubt, Smuts relied entirely on Henderson to direct the reorganization of the air services; and when the time came, the latter worked with great skill and energy to bring the R.A.F. into being.[21]

There can be no doubt that Henderson greatly influenced Smuts in the preparation of his report. Yet it is strange to say the least that Henderson should have actively assisted in the formulation of a policy whose principal feature was the formation of a strategic bomber force. However, this apparently inconsistent attitude can be explained quite simply. Henderson had for long believed that the correct allocation of air resources (which for him meant that the bulk of what was available should go to the tactical squadrons of the Flying Corps) could only be achieved if a single body with the necessary powers was created. He had witnessed what he considered to be the failure of the Joint War Air Committee and two Air Boards to achieve this. Now, two enemy raids on London – in themselves of no great military significance – had completely changed the situation. They had created a climate of opinion in which the Government might well be persuaded to set up a separate ministry. Sensing that this was a unique opportunity, Henderson urged Smuts to recommend this course of action, promising his support in the work of reorganization. It is unlikely he had suddenly become a convert to strategic bombing. Perhaps he felt it was a small price to pay for the new department of state. Or perhaps he had no more faith in Lord Cowdray's 'Surplus Aircraft Fleet' than Haig or Trenchard.

Though having approved in principle the recommendations of

the Smuts Report, the Cabinet postponed its decision on the creation of an air ministry. There was in truth no great enthusiasm for such a massive reorganization in wartime. The year 1917 was a black one for the allied cause, and the Government had difficulties in plenty without risking what many considered to be the certain disruption of the air services if the proposed changes were undertaken. But opinion both in Parliament and in the country was strongly in favour of a separate air service. It had come to identify the air reforms with the establishment of a new ministry, and would accept nothing less. After a brief hesitation, the Government yielded to the pressure. A bill was quickly drafted and, after a virtually unhindered passage through Parliament, it received the Royal Assent on 29th November 1917.[22]

In the first Air Council, which came into being in January 1918,[23] Lord Rothermere was the Secretary of State for the Air Force and General Trenchard, whom Sir Douglas Haig had reluctantly released from his post in France, was Chief of the Air Staff. Sir David Henderson was Additional Member and Vice-President. During the first three months of 1918 the Air Council worked at top pressure to bring the new service into existence. In spite of the immense effort which this task involved, Lord Rothermere found time to draw in outline a plan for the strategic offensive. However, he was not destined to see his ideas mature. From the first the Air Council was beset by internal dissension, for it soon became apparent that Lord Rothermere and Trenchard found it impossible to work together. The Official Historian commented tactfully on the situation:

It will be enough to say that Major-General Trenchard took a much wider view of the responsibilities of the Chief of the Air Staff than it appeared to him the Secretary of State was willing to accord, but it is clear, also, that there were differences of temperament.[24]

By the middle of March the situation had become intolerable, and Trenchard resigned. A month later Lord Rothermere also resigned. Lord Rothermere was replaced by Sir William Weir, the Director-General of Aircraft Production and a member of the first Air Council, and Trenchard by Major-General F.H. Sykes, who was then serving with the British section of the Supreme War Council at Versailles. As soon as Henderson was informed of the appointment of Sykes, he too resigned, on the ground that he could not work with the new Chief of the Air Staff.[25]

With the bulk of the work of re-organization completed, the new Air Council was free to devote more attention to the air offensive. Sir William Weir and General Sykes, both keen advocates of strategic bombing, already looked forward to the time when the British squadrons in Lorraine would be transformed into a powerful allied bombing force.[26] This vision was based on the expectation of a major contribution from the Americans. In May 1918 the first re-inforcements were despatched to the squadrons at Nancy, and on 6th June this force became officially known as the Independent Force.

* * *

At this point it will be convenient to return to the summer of 1917. As soon as the Government had accepted General Smuts' proposal for an air offensive, the Air Board called upon a number of experts to advise on the formulation of a bombing policy. Among the first to be consulted was Lord Tiverton, then serving with the naval section of the British Aviation Commission in Paris. He held the post of technical liaison officer with the French, with special responsibility for armaments.

It will be remembered that in 1915 Lord Tiverton had begun a detailed study of strategic bombing. His object was to discover what knowledge and skills were essential to success in this type of bombing, and in the light of his findings to determine the requirements of a bomber force in terms of aircraft, equipment, organization, and programmes of training and experimentation. One example, that of navigation, will illustrate his approach. His study of long distance flights quickly convinced him of the vital importance of accurate navigation, so he sought to find the best methods of navigation for day and night operations, the most suitable types of maps and instruments for use in the air, and the most efficient ways of training crews for this work. By mid-1917 he had formed an estimate of the nature of strategic operations which the history of the following twenty-five years shows to have been remarkably accurate.

But if the results of Lord Tiverton's work were outstanding, so was the method he used to obtain them. His invariable rule was to select the most reliable information, whether that was scientific data, evidence provided by experience, the results of experiments and tests, the results of mathematic calculations of probability, or a combination of these. He refused to use information based on estimates or opinions, no matter how reliable they were considered to be. His work anticipated by many years the method of scientific research which came to be known as Operational Research. His most impressive application of this method was in his calculations of the probable number of bombs required to destroy various kinds of targets. When Lord Tiverton left the Air Ministry at the end of the First World War his work was forgotten, and the methods which he had evolved were not applied to the solution of bombing problems until the initial failure of the bombing offensive in the Second World War.

Some time in August 1917 Lord Tiverton was requested by Captain V. Vyvyan, R.N. to submit to the Air Board a paper on bombing, covering any points he thought relevant. He was instructed to assume for the purpose of his report that a force of 2,000 aeroplanes would be available, that the principal aim of the offensive would be the systematic destruction of the German munition industry, and that the base for operations would be situated either in the Ostend region or in the area Verdun-Toul.[26]

In his paper, which was dated 3rd September 1917, Lord Tiverton first dealt with the question of targets. He drew up a list of possible objectives and divided them geographically into four groups. The first three were the industrial centres around the cities of Düsseldorf, Cologne and Mannheim; the fourth was the steel industry of the Saar Valley. Having established the location of the main targets, he then considered which of the two areas suggested to him was the more suitable as a base for operations. In view of the scheme he had in mind, there was in fact only one possible choice, the Verdun – Toul area. The outstanding disadvantage of operating from the Ostend region would be that of the four target groups he had selected only two of them, the Düsseldorf and Cologne groups, would be within range.

A further disadvantage [he stated] will be that the Germans will be quite aware of these facts, and, therefore, for the purposes of defence, they will know the limitations of the objectives on every raid, whereas in the Verdun/Toul base, they will never know for which particular objective a raid is intended, and hence will be proportionately extravagant of machines for defence purposes in a very difficult country, or else they will have to chance a meagre defence. Furthermore, any aeroplanes concentrated for the purpose of defence will be quite useless for any other purpose, whereas a concentration for defence from the Ostend district might be very useful for general purposes on the Western front.

Finally, a consideration of the frequency of suitable weather conditions for long-range operations seemed to Lord Tiverton to rule out the Ostend base.

There are only a certain number of days, very few and far between, on which it is possible to raid to the distance which is necessary for the first three groups of targets. On a liberal estimate, these will not be more than 4 or 5 per month during the summer months. There will, however, be a large percentage of days when short raids can be quite well carried out. In the Belgian district there is no objective for this *as part of a scheme for the systematic destruction of the German muniton works.* The Saar Valley with its steel works, offers exactly what is required as such an objective for days on which it is only possible to do short raids.

Lord Tiverton then considered whether operations should be carried out by day or night, for it should be noted that he did not plan for a force comprising both day and night bombers. Though this may seem a strange decision, it can be explained by his belief that such a large force, based in an area where communications were poor and roads and railways congested, could be most efficiently operated with one main type of bomber aircraft. His preference was for daylight operations because:

... the greatest moral effect is by day when the operatives are actively engaged in their work or in the streets without any particular place to go to, rather than by night when they are in their own houses where they have at any rate got a roof over their heads, a fact which gives a considerable moral sense of safety and a considerable practical factor of safety against stray shells from anti-aircraft fire.

He had however other reasons for rejecting night operations. First, navigation over long distances at night presented great difficulties and was restricted to those periods when conditions of weather and moonlight were favourable. Secondly, in a situation in which the production of aircraft was an important factor, an aeroplane as large as the Handley Page, the standard night bomber, required more material in its construction and took longer to build than the smaller day bomber, such as the D.H.9. In addition, the very size of the aircraft rendered difficult the transportation of spare parts in the area around Toul. A spare wing, for instance, was too tall to go under many bridges. Thirdly, the use of night bombers would entail an increase in the number of trained flying personnel, for the Handly Page carried a crew of three as against

K

two in the day bomber.

After dealing with other problems, such as supply, transport and accommodation, he then turned to considerations of a purely operational nature. One of the most important of these was the need for an efficient metereological service. Experience had shown that the weather in the Toul area was generally very different from that in the Rhine valley, and because of this, accurate and up-to-date weather reports were essential. Experience had also shown that these could only be satisfactorily prepared at the operational base.

Metereological officers should therefore be sent *at once* to study the weather conditions in that country from now until next spring when it is intended to commence operations.

Lord Tiverton next examined the problems of air navigation, and his remarks on this subject reveal how clearly he understood its importance as an element of long-distance bombing.

It cannot be recognized too early, that the problem of bombing over distances which vary between 150 and 200 miles necessitates a training in the knowledge of the country among the pilots which is far beyond anything which they are now given. It is not a question so much of theoretic navigation as of knowing the maps of the country over which they are going to fly so well that they have no difficulty in recognizing any possible outstanding mark that they may come across. This means months of training in those particular maps and not a few weeks training on the general reading of any maps. . . . Experience has shown that it is quite easy for five squadrons to set out to bomb a particular target and for only one of those five ever to reach the objective, while the other four, in the honest belief that they had done so, have bombed four different villages which bore little if any resemblance to the one they desired to attack.

Finally, Lord Tiverton considered the general plan of attack, and in outlining this, he emphasized the importance of concentration of effect in order to produce the greatest possible damage, both in terms of material and morale, as well as to hamper the defences.

> Therefore, it is suggested, that all available aeroplanes should concentrate on one objective on one day. For instance, suppose a hundred squadrons to be available and that it was desired to attack Mannheim and the Ludwigshafen works — assuming a timetable of three minutes between the squadrons this would amount to a bombardment of five continuous hours. If Frankfort were attacked later in a similar way it is quite possible that Cologne would create such trouble that the German Government might be forced to suggest terms before that town was attacked. Further, after such a bombardment, the main works would be wrecked and the moral of the operatives shattered.

Meanwhile, General Trenchard had, after difficult and protracted negotiations, secured from the French a base for operations at Ochey,[28] near Nancy. He had found the French authorities most reluctant to grant him the aerodrome accommodation he required, for they were strongly opposed to the British plan to attack German cities.[29]

The reason for their opposition was without doubt the serious depression of morale throughout France following the disastrous failure of the Nivelle offensive in the spring of 1917. The shock of this defeat, in which casualties were very heavy, was felt throughout the French Army. Mutinies broke out among the front-line troops and these quickly spread to other units, until over half the French Army was involved.[30] Nor was the disaffection confined to the Army; there was widespread unrest among the civilian population and in many industrial centres workers went on strike.

After Nivelle's dismissal, General Pétain was appointed Commander-in-Chief, and he at once addressed himself to the task of restoring the nation's confidence in its ability to win the war. To this end, he determined that no large-scale offensive action should be undertaken along the French front until discipline and morale had been restored among the troops. He was much concerned too with morale among the French civilian population, and when the British air offensive was proposed he feared that the Germans might retaliate with attacks upon French cities. Without doubt, the opposition which Trenchard encountered in his search for bases was directly connected with Pétain's resolve to remain on the defensive until the damage caused by the Nivelle offensive had been repaired.

Indeed, Pétain left the British in no doubt as to his views on this subject. In September he wrote to Sir Douglas Haig suggesting that bombing in the northern sector of the front should be confined to enemy aerodromes, since the present policy of attacking various objectives behind the enemy lines incited the Germans to make raids on such places as Dunkirk, Calais and Boulogne. The enemy raids on Dunkirk, he pointed out, were creating so serious a situation that the dockers were threatening to leave the town.

In his reply, Haig stated that he could not agree to the proposal, but Pétain had no intention of letting the matter rest. A few days later he again raised the question of bombing and its effects on civilians. This time he told Haig that he had issued orders prohibiting French aircraft from making light, scattered raids on German towns, on the grounds that these would probably have no other effect than 'to provoke reprisals on French towns, or at least furnish a pretext for them . . .'. He therefore asked that similar instructions should be given to British squadrons. Haig however refused to commit himself to a firm promise, though he acknowledged that he agreed in principle with the suggestion.[31]

However, in spite of their opposition to the bombing plan, the French did not prevent the British from obtaining a base for operations in the zone under their control. On the other hand, they were prepared to give no more than the minimum of assistance, and even that was given reluctantly. Though Trenchard did obtain aerodrome accommodation at Ochey, this was sufficient only for his most immediate needs. And in any case, the arrangement was not a permanent one, for the French expected the aerodrome to be returned to them in the spring of 1918. In fact, the temporary loan of the Ochey base was very nearly as far as the French were prepared extend their co-operation. They firmly refused to grant facilities on aerodromes already constructed, but finally offered to provide land on which new aerodromes could be built. Trenchard accepted this offer, and though the 'ridge and furrow' of the Nancy area was difficult country for such work, he was able to report at the end of November 1917 that the construction of two aerodromes had already begun.[3 2]

At the beginning of October Trenchard received orders to begin the bombing of targets in Germany, and he at once formed the 41st Wing specifically for that purpose. Three squadrons were allocated to the wing and these were No. 55 (D.H.4) for day bombing; and No. 100 (F.E.2b) and No. 16 Naval Squadron (Handley Page) for night bombing.[3 3] Circumstances could hardly have been less favourable for an offensive against Germany. In the first place, the force was too small for such an undertaking, and this weakness was accentuated by the fact that only two of the aircraft types, the D.H.4 and the Handley Page, had sufficient range to reach the German objectives. Secondly, the season of the year was then approaching when long-distances operations would be severely restricted by unfavourable weather conditions.

It was perhaps with these considerations in mind that the commander-in-chief of the French armies of the north and north-east wrote to Sir Douglas Haig requesting the co-operation of the newly-formed wing in the revised French bombing plan. It must not be thought that the French had suspended the bombing of all enemy targets. Their intention was to avoid attacking those objectives, in particular German cities, which they believed would bring retaliatory raids against their own cities. It will be remembered that in March 1917 the French had produced a plan which concentrated all bombing activity against the iron pro-ducing regions of the Saar, Luxembourg and Lorraine. At first they carried out a general attack against the iron works in these areas, but their bomber strength was not sufficient to effect a serious reduction of the output of iron ore.

As a result of the limited success achieved by this method of attack, the General Staff held a review of their bombing policy and decided to concentrate on the railways of Lorraine and Luxembourg, along which the iron ore was transported to Germany. They believed that a systematic bombardment of the main railway stations on the periphery of the iron producing areas would disrupt the flow of iron ore into Germany more effectively than raids on individual iron works. They therefore drew up a modified bombing plan, and among the chief targets listed were the stations at Luxembourg, Athus, Longuyon, Conflans, Metz, Thionville and Bettembourg.

This then was the plan in which the British were asked to participate. In his reply Haig stated that although the British force had been created chiefly to carry out 'long-range attacks on German commercial towns as reprisals for enemy air raids on Allied towns', there would be occasions when co-operation would be possible; for example, during the early period when the British airmen were making themselves familiar with the countryside, and, later, when weather conditions precluded raids into Germany.[34]

When the wing began to operate in October 1917 the number of raids that could be made against German targets was severely restricted both by the limited operational capability of the force and by adverse weather conditions. The raids were not based on any bombing programme, and this is hardly surprising, since the majority of the targets it was desired to attack were not at that time operationally feasible. As a result, the choice of targets during the winter of 1917-18 was for the most part left to the French whose bombing plan concentrated on objectives which were at short range from the Nancy base.

When at the end of summer the threat of further daylight raids seemed to have passed, the Government began to have second thoughts concerning its commitment to a strategic bombing campaign. It was felt that this involvement had become much greater than had originally been intended. What had started as a simple idea for retaliatory raids against German cities had developed into a plan for a full-scale offensive against the enemy war-effort. This had come about principally because the scheme for retaliatory raids had become identified with General Smuts' proposals for a bombing campaign and the re-organization of the air services. Indeed, the Government itself was somewhat slow in drawing a distinction between the two and in consequence committed itself more deeply than it would have wished. When therefore the Cabinet re-considered its acceptance of the Smuts recommendations opinion had swung the other way. In particular there was general opposition to the setting-up of a separate air department in wartime.

Meanwhile, the ardent supporters of strategic bombing waited impatiently for the Government to put into effect its promised air policy. One of these was Rear-Admiral Mark Kerr, who had been appointed to the Air Board after returning from command of the British Adriatic Squadron in August 1917. Admiral Kerr rated air power of first importance, believing that the swiftest way to deal the enemy a crippling blow was to attack his war industries with long-range aircraft. These aircraft, he was convinced, should be organized as an independent bombing force, operating under the control of an air ministry which he had every reason to believe the Government intended to establish.

On 10th October Admiral Kerr discovered the reality of the situation. On that day he was informed by Lord Cowdray, President of the Air Board, that it was almost certain the Government would decide against an independent bombing force.[35] The implication of that was clear: there would be no air ministry either. On the same day, Admiral Kerr received a private letter from Lord Tiverton in France, warning him that almost nothing had been done to prepare for the reception of the bomber force in the Verdun-Toul district. Especially serious, Lord Tiverton pointed out, was the fact that no arrangements had been put in hand to provide the necessary road and rail transport, without which no real progress could be made.[36]

Admiral Kerr needed no further indication as to how matters stood. He at once sent a strongly-worded memorandum to Lord Cowdray, urging 'the extraordinary danger of delay in forming the Air Ministry and commencing on a proper Air Policy'. His study of the enemy air position had convinced him that the Germans were preparing for a large-scale air offensive against England. To this end they were building a fleet of four thousand large bombing machines. In addition they had already brought into service a new powerful bomber with many times the carrying capacity of the Gotha. All this, Admiral Kerr emphasized, amounted to a serious threat to Britain.

It is, [he wrote] a race between them and us; every day lost is a vital danger. If the Germans get at us first, with several hundred machines every night, each one carrying several tons of explosives, Woolwich, Chatham and all the factories in the London district will be laid flat, part of London wiped out, and workshops in the south-east of England will be destroyed, and consequently our offensive on land, sea, and air will come to an end.

There is no exaggeration in this, and if we are going to stop it, we must start at once with our preparations to lay their factories flat, and to destroy their aerodromes. This will entail the building of 2000 big bombing machines as a minimum, the training of pilots, the preparation of aerodromes, the building of sheds, manufacture of bombs, the collection of transport, all of which will take about five months to complete.

In short, it means the country who first strikes with its big bombing squadrons of hundreds of machines at the enemy's vital spots, will win the war.[37]

The memorandum was at once communicated to the members of the Cabinet. Though its estimate of the enemy's air capacity was much higher than that suggested by other sources of information — it was in fact greatly exaggerated — the Government was reluctant to ignore such a categorical warning. The memorandum was discussed at a meeting of the Cabinet, and the question of air policy was again brought to the fore. It is difficult to imagine anything that would have troubled the Government more than a prediction, emanating from a responsible quarter, of large-scale air attacks on London. This unease was expressed by Lloyd George when he told Trenchard that the Germans were going to bomb London with four thousand aeroplanes. Trenchard, with his customary bluntness replied, 'Nonsense, forty'.[38]

Nevertheless, the fear persisted that the seemingly impossible figure might prove to be the correct one. In this uncertainty of mind the Government was assailed by widespread pressures to implement the recommendations of the Smuts Report. While it cannot be pretended that Admiral Kerr's memorandum caused the Government to change its policy, it is true to say that it prepared opinion in the Cabinet in such a way as to make the change politically easier than it would otherwise have been.

An immediate result of the Cabinet's discussions was the setting up of the Air Policy Committee, under the chairmanship of General Smuts. The functions of the committee, whose members were the First Lord of the Admiralty, the Secretary of State for War and the President of the Air Board, were to formulate air policy and advise the Cabinet until such time as the air ministry came into being. In addition, the committee was almost certainly intended to assume the functions of the air ministry if, as was by no means unlikely, the Government decided to abandon its plans for air re-organization. However, the crucial question was settled once for all when Parliament re-assembled after the summer recess, on 16th October. The Commons was in no mood to tolerate further delay in the air reforms, and Bonar Law, yielding to the will of the House, gave an undertaking that the Government would take action without delay. 'A Bill,' he announced, 'to constitute an Air Ministry has been prepared and will shortly be introduced.'[3][9]

Trouble came soon and from an unexpected quarter. On 16th November there appeared in *The Times* a letter from Lord Northcliffe to the Prime Minister. In it Lord Northcliffe explained his reasons for being unable to accept the Prime Minister's offer of the post of air minister. This was the first intimation that many of the Prime Minister's colleagues received that such an offer had been made. To one of these, Lord Cowdray, who had hopes that he himself might be invited to take control of the new air department, the manner in which the affair had been conducted caused great offence, and he at once resigned.[40] This was a difficult period. 'We struggle daily to overcome inertia with varying success. . . .' wrote Admiral Kerr at the Air Board to Lord Tiverton, on 22nd November.[41]

By the end of the month, however, the corner seemed to have been turned. The new minister, Lord Rothermere, had taken up his duties and Admiral Kerr noted with relief: 'I really believe we are putting a move on at last.'[42]

Early in November Lord Tiverton forwarded to the Air Board the second of his two papers on bombing.[43] In the covering letter, addressed to Admiral Kerr, he expressed the hope that he would soon be re-called to London (he was still serving with the British Aviation Commission in Paris) to help with the work of planning the offensive. This paper was devoted entirely to the selection of targets, and employed that method of scientific analysis (later known as Operational Research) of which mention has already been made. Here it was used to make an assessment of the vulnerability of nearly a hundred German factories manufacturing war materials.

As a basis for his work Lord Tiverton assumed that of the two thousand aircraft in the bombing force (the figure he was instructed to use in the first paper) one thousand would be available at any given time to attack a specific target. With the load of each aircraft assumed to be nine bombs, a total of nine thousand bombs could be directed against any target. For each individual target, the area occupied by the factory was calculated and an assessment (based on the nature of the manufacturing activities) was made of the area occupied by buildings and plant vulnerable to bomb attack. Making an allowance for mean bombing errors considerably more than twice the mean errors for practice bomb-dropping in England, Lord Tiverton calculated, among other things, the probable number of bombs to fall within the factory area and the probable number of bombs that would cause effective damage.

To illustrate the kind of results obtained by this method, two examples will be taken from the list of chemical works: one, a large factory of 168 acres, the Badische Anilin und Soda Fabrik at Ludwigshafen; the other, a small factory of 23 acres, the Casella at Frankfurt. Calculations indicated that in the case of the Badische works 84% of the bombs would have fallen within the factory area, as against 14% for the Casella; and as to the probable number of bombs causing effective damage, the figure was 4150 out of 9000 (46%) for the Badische works compared with 225 out of 9000 (2.8%) for the Casella. If these probabilities of bombing achievement were restated in terms of the number of bombs that would have to be dropped to ensure that at least one would be effective the figures were even more striking: an average of 11 bombs would have to be dropped on the Badische works as against 225 for the Casella.

The conclusions which Lord Tiverton drew from his analysis of targets confirmed what study and experience had already taught him. In the first place, all the statistics pointed to the need for attacks on a large scale if worthwhile damage was to be achieved. Large factories were easy to hit but difficult to destroy: small factories were easy to destroy but difficult to hit. The best plan, Lord Tiverton believed, was to launch a bombing campaign with the firm intention of destroying completely (Lord Tiverton used the word 'obliterating') the chosen targets and not merely causing damage which could easily be repaired. Secondly, targets must be selected with great care so that the bombing produced the greatest disruptive effect on the German war effort. If the second aim was to be achieved an exhaustive study of the supply and demand of war materials in Germany would have to be undertaken so that enemy weaknesses could be revealed and exploited.

Lord Tiverton had little doubt in which area Germany was most vulnerable.

> The most important perhaps of all targets because they are few in number and particularly vulnerable, both from reasons of size and contents, are the chemical works. The supply of nitrates in Germany is largely kept up by synthetic processes and an attack upon these would largely paralyse the explosive industries.

Though he listed seven factories as being the most important ones, he recognized that of these three in particular were in a class by themselves. These were the Badische Anilin und Soda Fabrik at Ludwigshafen, the Meister Lucius at Höchst and the Bayer at Cologne. Lord Tiverton believed that given

> a total available force at any one time of 1000 aeroplanes, each carrying nine bombs and if a campaign were started at the beginning of next April with these three targets in view, the German chemical industry might be crippled by the middle of May, provided that ordinary weather conditions prevailed and that the rest of the organization were taken in hand in time.

In addition to the chemical works the survey of targets included, among others, factories manufacturing explosives, aero-engines and magnetos, and iron and steel. Though producing war material of vital importance, the explosive factories had little attraction for Lord Tiverton as targets. They were constructed in such a way that any explosion occuring during the process of manufacture could be confined to that part of the factory in which it originated, and this feature of their design rendered them particularly difficult targets to damage by bombing.

> The percentage of vulnerable points, [Lord Tiverton noted] in relation to the acreage of actual works is extremely small and therefore it is evidently better to strangle these by attacking the chemical works which feed them, rather than attacking them directly.

The aero-engine and magneto industries, which were dealt with together, were considered hardly less important than the chemical industry. Unfortunately, almost nothing was known of the extent to which they had expanded since the war, by the use of new or converted factories. It was virtually certain that the main pre-war firms, like their counterparts in the allied countries, would make use of a large number of sub-contractors to increase output. This expedient was possible in these two industries since the majority of components used for aero-engines and magnetos could be produced in factories not originally designed for the work, provided the necessary machinery was available. In these circumstances, it would be most difficult to select a limited number of centres whose destruction would cripple, or even seriously effect, the industries.

Finally, the section on the iron and steel industries included a long list of plants both in Germany and in the occupied territories. Their chief importance for Lord Tiverton was a geographical one: the majority of them lay within short range of the allied aerodromes and could be attacked when weather conditions precluded flights against long-distance targets. For this reason they must of necessity be included in any bombing scheme.

Another paper on strategic bombing which is worthy of note

was submitted to the Air Board in December 1917 by the
Admiralty. The paper was written by Wing Commander C.J.R.
Randall, a naval air staff officer, but it is clear that the ideas
expressed in it reflected the policy of the Air Department and
were not merely the views of one officer.[44] Wing Commander
Randall began by defining the primary object of any offensive
against the enemy. It was, he stated, 'to take away his power of
initiating action, that is to say, to put him on the defensive and
prevent him from assuming the offensive at any point'. If such an
effect could be produced, it would, he believed, be decisive in
bringing the war to a successful conclusion. The question to which
an answer was required was which, if any, of the forms of air
bombing could achieve this. He first disposed of the bombing of
open towns which he did not consider a very effective means of
attack. This type of bombing might 'cause a panic among the
civilian population' and so strengthen the desire for peace in the
enemy country, but there was the possibility (a prophetic
suggestion in the light of events in the Second World War) that 'if
any particular towns were bombed consistently, over a protracted
period, the population would probably get used to being bombed'.

Nor would the tactical use of aircraft prove any more effective.
Bombing operations in support of the army involved attacks
against various targets in the immediate vicinity of the front.

> Owing to the length of the front, [he wrote] and the
> comparatively small number of bombing aircraft per mile of
> front, operations of this nature, though they will produce
> temporary inconvenience to the enemy in his conduct of the
> war, are not likely to produce any decisive results.

Even when the bombing was extended a considerable distance
behind the front line the results were no more impressive.
Similarly, bombing attacks against enemy surface vessels and
submarines were purely naval operations and could not bring
about a decisive result.

There was in fact only one type of bombing, Wing Commander Randall believed, which could have a decisive influence on the enemy's ability to continue the war, namely, attacks upon the various factories in which the vital munitions of war were produced. His statement justifying this belief is worthy to be quoted in full.

The advantage of this over attacking ammunition dumps etc. near the front is that the factories where the munitions are made, can, in most cases, be easily located, and further that the actual material is in the form in which it can be most easily destroyed. In attacking munition works of this description the main object should be to destroy all enemy sources of supply of some one or more essential munitions of war, without which his other war industries would be greatly hampered, or else rendered useless. For instance, if the whole of his production of high explosive can be stopped, the need to attack those factories in which he is making guns, shells etc, at once disappears. In the same way, by stopping the supply of aero-engines the necessity for destroying the actual aeroplane works is done away with.

If however this type of bombing was to be attempted, careful consideration must be given to the selection of industries to discover which of them could most easily be destroyed. It was essential that the factories in the selected industries should conform to certain requirements. They should be large targets, easy to locate from the air by day and night, be vulnerable to attack by bombs, and be one of a small number of large factories producing the same material. Wing Commander Randall examined in detail the types of factories engaged in manufacturing the most important materials and then drew up a list, in order of priority, of the objectives that should be attacked. The first four groups on this list were as follows: chemical and explosive factories; accumulator works manufacturing batteries for submarines; aero-engine and magneto works; iron and steel works.

Meanwhile, the Air Policy Committee, in consultation with its expert advisers, was preparing a general plan for the expansion and employment of the bomber force during 1918. The results of these deliberations were embodied in a memorandum circulated early in January 1918.[45] With regard to the expansion of the bomber force, the aims to be held in view were at any rate clearly set out. It was emphasized that there was an acute shortage of aerodrome accommodation in the vicinity of Nancy and that serious technical problems were involved in creating new aerodromes in the difficult terrain of that region.

However, measures to improve the situation were well in hand. Five new aerodromes were at that time being constructed and these were expected to provide accommodation for twenty-five squadrons by the beginning of May. Accommodation for a further fifteen squadrons was hoped to be completed by the beginning of July, with a further, but unspecified, increase in accommodation soon after that. Every effort, too, was to be made to expand the force as quickly as possible, the first three additional squadrons being scheduled to arrive before 30th April. After that date, reinforcements were to be provided every month, so that there would be ten additional squadrons by the end of June, twenty-three by the end of August, and thirty-one by the end of October.

Operational policy on the other hand was less clearly formulated. The memorandum stated that in accordance with the instructions issued by the War Cabinet raids upon industrial towns on or near the Rhine were being carried out whenever possible.

But these long distances are only possible when weather conditions are exceptionally favourable, and these machines cannot be expected, even under very suitable conditions, to go further than Mannheim. When long distance bombing is not possible short distance targets are attacked, such as Briey or Saarebruck, with a view to knocking out the enemy's steel manufactures. The selection of these short distance targets is

Pilot and Observer of a Handley Page 0/400 of No. 207 Squadron RAF, 1918.
Note the drift sight attached to the nose of the aircraft.
(*Photo: Imperial War Museum*).

Handley Page 0/100 of No. 14 Squadron RNAS, Coudekerque (near Dunkirk) 1918.
Damaged by AA fire.
(*Photo: J. M. Bruce: G. S. Leslie Collection*)

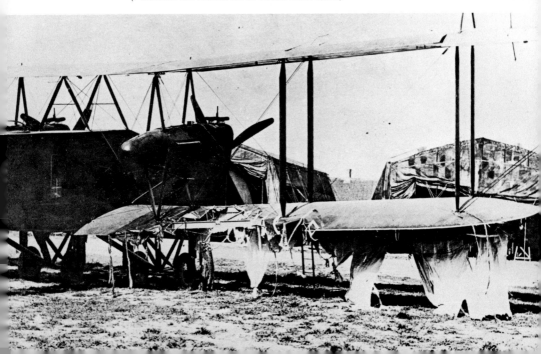

Handley Page 0/400.
(*Photo: J. M. Bruce: G. S. Leslie Collection*).

DH4 day bomber.
(*Photo: Imperial War Museum*).

left to the French so that the closest co-operation is secured between the Allies in this work.

It was made clear that the numerical weakness of the force was the chief factor in determining the objectives to be attacked, and this situation could not be changed until the three squadrons at Nancy had been transformed into a force of much greater striking power. And when such a force should be assembled, the Air Policy Committee was in no doubt as to how it should be used.

The policy intended to be followed, [the memorandum stated] is to attack the important German towns systematically, having regard to weather conditions and the defensive arrangements of the enemy. It is intended to concentrate on one town for successive days and then to pass to several other towns, returning to the first town until the target is thoroughly destroyed, or at any rate until the morale of workmen is so shaken that output is seriously interfered with.

The Committee regarded the forthcoming air campaign as a battle which must be won or lost. If victory was to be achieved, the offensive must be carried out systematically, in accordance with a definite plan, and fought with the utmost determination in the face of all difficulties.

Long distance bombing will produce its maximum moral effect only if the visits are constantly repeated at short intervals, so as to produce in each area bombed a sustained anxiety. It is this recurrent bombing, as opposed to isolated and spasmodic attacks, which interrupts industrial production and undermines public confidence. On the other hand, if the enemy were to succeed in interrupting the continuity of the British bombing operations, their achievements (as the Allies success against Zeppelins shew) that it would be an

L

immense encouragement to them which would operate like a military victory.

Having thus stated the operational aims of the offensive, the memorandum ended with the warning that arrangements must be completed in advance to make good instantly the heavy lossess that would inevitably occur.

In view of the fact that strategic bombing, as developed by the Admiralty, was based on the principle of an attack upon the enemy war effort, it is remarkable that the memorandum contained no hint of a plan for attacking German war industries. Indeed, the Committee's thinking on the question of bombing policy had not progressed beyond a statement of the general method of attack to be employed against large German cities. It is true that a list of possible targets was appended to the memorandum, but since this contained objectives in nearly a hundred and fifty cities in Germany and German occupied territory, it could not in any sense of the word be called a plan.

Another notable feature of the memorandum was the emphasis placed upon an offensive policy, and both this and the absence of a definite bombing plan may be traced directly to the influence of Trenchard who, as Chief of the Air Staff elect, had frequently been consulted by the Committee. In fact, the last passage quoted from the memorandum was taken almost verbatim from a paper prepared by Trenchard's headquarters in November 1917.[46] In this paper, entitled 'Long Distance Bombing', Trenchard made much of his belief that if the desired material and morale damage were to be inflicted upon the enemy, the bombing must be sustained and aggressive. It is also clear that he considered the effect on morale at least as important as material damage, if not more so. In other words, he did not regard the destruction of the enemy's vital war industries as the principal aim of the bombing offensive. From this point of view, the best way of causing both types of damage was to direct heavy and sustained attacks against large industrial centres, irrespective of whether the targets in these centres formed part of a particular industry or group of industries. For this reason, the statement on bombing made no mention of a plan for attacking enemy industry, merely referring to German war industry as one of several desirable types of objectives.

This was perhaps the first statement of the doctrine which was to dominate strategic thought in the Royal Air Force from the early post-war period until the middle of the Second World War. This doctrine was the work of Trenchard and represented the peace-time counterpart of his wartime offensive policy. The air defence of Britain was vested in a home-based force of bombers which, in the event of an attack upon this country, would be launched against the populous centres of the enemy.

This concept of defence through strategic air action was based on the principle that if the selected targets were situated in large industrial areas even the bombs which failed to hit the aiming points would injure the morale of the enemy workers by destroying their lives and homes and disrupting the public services (water, gas, transport and so on) on which they depended. It seemed to offer a method of attack by which every bomb dropped could be made to count, thus creating an exaggerated notion of the destructive effect of air bombing, it also led to an unwarranted complacency regarding operational standards, and this in turn obscured the need to investigate the problems of defence against enemy fighters and guns and to improve the methods of navigation, target location, and bomb-aiming.

It did not occur to the air staffs of the inter-war period that, over long distances, bombers might be prevented from reaching their targets, in daylight by the action of enemy fighters and ground defences, and at night by their own inability to locate even quite large towns in conditions of wartime blackout. In truth, the consideration of such problems did not out live the air staff of 1918.

* * *

Meanwhile, the three squadrons of the 41st Wing at Nancy which Admiral Kerr described as 'the detachment from the B.E.F.' had begun operations in the middle of October. It was a makeshift force and its operations were organized on makeshift lines. No meteorological service had been established, there were few suitable maps and no navigational instruments and nothing had been done to provide adequate briefing for the crews.

Operations began, on 17th October, with a daylight raid by the D.H.4's of No. 55 Squadron against the Burbach iron works near Saarbrücken. Eight of the eleven aircraft which set out bombed the target and damage was caused to the plant. Night operations did not, however, begin so auspiciously. Weather conditions were poor on the evening of 24th October when naval Handley Pages and F.E.2b's of No. 100 Squadron carried out attacks on the Burbach iron works and on targets along the railway line between Falkenburg and Saarbrucken. Two Handley Pages and two F.E.2b's failed to return.

When Captain C.L. Lambe, commander of the naval squadrons at Dunkirk, visited No. 16 Naval Squadron he was far from happy at the situation there. He reported to the Vice-Admiral Dover Patrol:

Of the ten machines which were sent down, five are out of action. Two have been reported 'missing', one completely wrecked, and two damaged and cannot be made serviceable until spares are provided from England.

Captain Lambe had no doubt as to the cause of this state of affairs.

It is regretted that on the first raid three machines out of ten have been lost, together with the occupants of two of them, but I would strongly emphasize that it is most inadvisable to hurriedly collect together machines, pilots and personnel and use the same as an Active Service Squadron. After two years experience, I feel convinced that to obtain good results with a minimum of loss it is absolutely necessary for a squadron to be thoroughly trained.[47]

For the remainder of 1917 weather conditions continued to be bad, especially for night operations. During the months of November and December only five raids were possible. The last raid of the year, on 24th December, was the first successful attempt to reach Mannheim. Ten D.H.4's of No. 55 Squadron attacked the city and caused damage to industrial workshops. During the first three months of 1918, weather conditions still restricted long-distance operations, but, though the strength of the wing still remained at three squadrons, the raids were generally more successful than during the preceding period of 1917. For the most part, the raids were made against factories, workshops and railways at short range. As in 1917, weather conditions were difficult for night flying, and the majority of the long-distance flights were carried out by day. At the end of this period, when the independent air service officially came into being, the D.H.4's had bombed targets in the German cities of Karlsruhe, Mainz, Stuttgart, Coblenz, Freiburg and Mannheim.[48]

It will be remembered that the need for a bombsight which was simple to operate in the air had been seen to be urgent as early as the summer of 1916. During the heavy air fighting of that period, the enemy's greater concentration on anti-aircraft defences had considerably increased the hazards involved in bombing operations. Pilots were more frequently under fire when they approached their targets, and in consequence, found the operation of the current bombsights unacceptably complicated. The setting of both the standard bombsights, the CFS4 and the equal-distance sight, necessitated a timed run in order to determine the ground-speed of the aircraft, and it was this measurement that was almost impossible to perform accurately under operational conditions. What was needed therefore was a sight which could be set without the use of a stop watch or any other mechanical timing device. And this requirement was fulfilled in the two 'drift' sights, the Low Height Bombsight and the High Altitude Bombsight, which were designed by Lieutenant-Commander H.E. Wimperis.[49] Both these sights, which were based on the same principle and were very similar in design, used an airspeed setting with an adjustment for wind speed. (See Figure 4, p. 167).

The Wimperis 'drift' sight was provided with three sighting bars, namely, one movable foresight, and two movable backsights set in a fixed position in relation to each other. The foresight moved vertically and was set to the height of the aircraft, while the two backsights moved horizontally and were set to the airspeed as shown by the airspeed indicator. Since the sight was intended to be used either up wind or down wind, the wind speed was then applied to the airspeed in order to obtain two ground-speeds: one for bombing with the wind, shown by the rear backsight, and the other for bombing into the wind, shown by the front backsight. This was in fact an addition or subtraction of the wind speed and was done automatically when the wind speed was set on the instrument. The arrangement of the sight to enable this to be carried out was as follows. A wind scale was fitted at right angles to the tube which carried the two backsights, and the pointer which moved along the wind scale was attached to a drift bar which in turn was connected to the two backsights. Therefore, when the wind speed pointer was set against the appropriate figure on the wind scale, the motion was transmitted by means of the drift bar to the two backsights which were then set to ground-speed.

It will be seen that the backsights could be set in one of two ways. Either the wind speed obtained from the meteorological service could be set on the wind scale or the drift bar could be aligned with the observed drift of the aircraft. It should be noted that the drift bar was so positioned as to record drift when the aircraft was flying directly across wind. If the pilot wished to set the instrument by means of a drift observation he had to carry out

LOW-HEIGHT BOMBSIGHT MK. II (Drift Pattern)

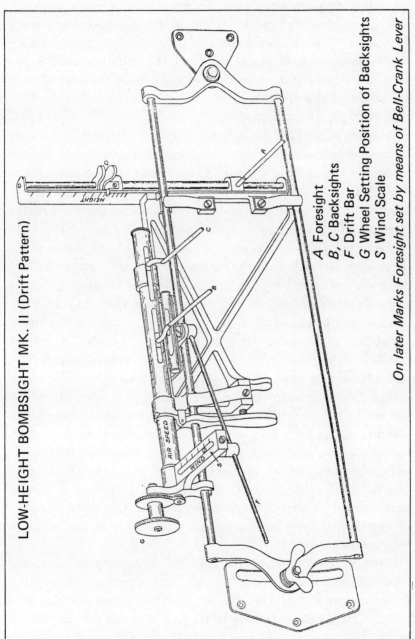

A Foresight
B, C Backsights
F Drift Bar
G Wheel Setting Position of Backsights
S Wind Scale

On later Marks Foresight set by means of Bell-Crank Lever

(Figure 4)

the following procedure. First, he steered the aircraft so that it was flying directly up or down wind, whichever was more convenient. Then, having made a 90° alteration of course to bring the aircraft across wind, he adjusted the drift bar until it was parallel to the apparent motion of objects on the ground. The movement of the drift bar during the observation determined the correct setting of the backsights.

In order to prepare the sight for bombing, the pilot first set the forecast wind speed against the wind scale or made a drift observation as described above. Then, having levelled the sight at the height at which he proposed to bomb, he set the foresight to height and the backsights to airspeed. On the approach to the target, the pilot sighted along the foresight and the front backsight if flying up wind, and along the foresight and rear backsight if flying down wind. As soon as the pilot observed the target to be in line with the upper edges of the two sights he released the bomb.

By the summer of 1917 the High Altitude Drift (H.A.D.) sight was in production, and after satisfactory trials by the naval squadrons at Dunkirk, was adopted by the R.N.A.S. as the standard sight for high level work. Soon afterwards the R.F.C., too, obtained a new sight, the negative lens sight, which was, within a short time, fitted to a large number of military aircraft. It was set in the floor of the aircraft, and this enabled the pilot to take his sight for bombing without assuming an awkward position. Its outstanding advantage was that it was simple to operate. In addition, pilots found the sight useful as a view finder and direction indicator. Though, in respect of accuracy, it was no improvement on previous sights, the negative lens sight is worthy of mention, if only because it was produced in greater numbers than any other sight.[50]

There were two parts to the sight.[51] The upper part, which was fitted in the floor of the cockpit, was a rectangular negative (plano-concave) lens through which four sighting wires were visible. One wire was parallel to the centre line of the aircraft, the other three were at right angles to it. Of these three wires, the one nearest to the front of the aircraft was marked with the figure '15', the middle one with the figure '10', and the rear one with the figure '6'. These figures represented heights in thousands of feet, with an indicated airspeed assumed for each height, thus: 15,000 feet at 70 m.p.h., 10,000 feet at 80 m.p.h., and 6,000 feet at 90 m.p.h. The air speeds were chosen as being average speeds for the D.H.4 when flying level at the three heights, the D.H.4 being the first aircraft to be fitted with this sight. The wires marked with these numbers were the backsights for the heights indicated. The lower part of the sight was set in the under side of the aircraft and was positioned below and slightly in front of the negative lens. This consisted of a fore and aft sighting wire, a range sighting wire at right angles to the fore and aft wire, and a scale along which the range sighting wire could be moved. The scale was marked with wind speeds from 0 to 40 m.p.h. at the three heights inscribed on the negative lens, zero for all heights being in the centre of the scale. For an up wind attack the range sighting wire was moved along the scale towards the rear of the aircraft; for a down wind attack it was moved along the scale to the front. The range sighting wire, which served as the foresight, was adjusted to the correct height/wind speed setting before each flight. The sight was designed either for up wind or down wind attacks and the pilot took as his line of sight the range sighting wire and the appropriate wire on the negative lens. The bomb was released when the target crossed this line of sight.

Finally, brief mention must be made of the course-setting bombsight, without doubt the most advanced sight produced during the war.[52] Designed by Lieutenant-Commander Wimperis in 1917, it proved most successful during trials at the naval seaplane base, Isles of Scilly, in December of that year. However, this bombsight properly belongs to the history of the post-war period, for it was produced only in small numbers during 1918 and never came into squadron service before the end of hostilities. In general arrangement it resembled the low height bombsights, Mks II and III, having a horizontal member graduated in airspeeds

and a vertical member graduated in heights. It was also fitted with
a wind scale and a drift bar. The feature which distinguished it
from all other previous sights was the incorporation into the
design of a small compass which enabled bombing to be carried
out in any direction relative to the wind. The course-setting
bombsight continued to be used in the R.A.F. for many years and
in a modified version was the standard bombsight in use at the
beginning of the Second World War.

The Government's decision to undertake a long-range bombing
campaign against Germany necessitated a radical improvement in
the standard of flying training given to military personnel. Judged
by any standards, the training given to R.F.C. pilots and observers
up to the end of 1917 was insufficient even for general service in
the field. But as an introduction to the highly specialized work of
long-distance flying it was hopelessly inadequate. It was not until
the adoption of naval methods of training during the early part of
1918, when the two services were in the process of amalgamation,
that a marked improvement was achieved.

One reason for the low standard of training was the constant
pressure placed upon the training schools to produce the ever
increasing numbers of pilots and observers needed to sustain the
offensive policy. But the main reason was that the military air
leaders never really understood the nature of the technical skills in
which it was necessary to train a pilot or observer for operational
duties. For example, no training was given in navigation or bomb
dropping, since it was assumed that such proficiency as was
required in these skills could be gained by actual operational
experience.

This attitude even extended to basic pilot training. The pilot
received no more than the most elementary instruction during
training and had to learn the techniques of flying an operational
aircraft while over the lines, often with disastrous consequences.[53]
As late as the spring of 1917 the average flying experience gained
by R.F.C. pilots before going overseas was only 17½ hours.[54]
Observer training was no better, and although a syllabus of

instruction had been laid down in August 1915, this was seldom followed. Like the pilots, the observers did not begin to acquire the essential skills of their work until reaching their operational squadrons. On the other hand, naval air training had early been placed on a sound footing. By the summer of 1916, a naval pilot attained something in the region of twenty-four hours solo at an elementary training school before going on to an advanced flying course to complete his training. After that, he received special training either in bombing tactics or air fighting, according to the type of squadron for which he was destined. Naval observers were trained at Eastchurch and their course lasted for four months.[55]

As was to be expected, the suggestion to introduce specialized training to meet the requirements of long-distance flying was first made by the Admiralty. Arrangements were made on the initiative of the Director of Air Services to establish a course in navigation at the Admiralty Compass Observatory at Slough. The course, which was designed for officers of both the air services, provided instruction in the use of compasses and in the practice of navigation on 'long distance flights over sea and over land at high altitudes, by day and night, when ground objects are not visible'.[56] This was only the beginning. The next step was to inaugurate a combined course of navigation and bombing, with facilities for practical training. This was established near Salisbury in January 1918, and the unit responsible for the training was called No. 1 School of Navigation and Bomb-Dropping, Stonehenge. Instruction was provided for pilots and observers, both of day and night bombers, and the subjects taught were compasses and navigation, gunnery, bombing, meteorology and aerial photography.[57] Thus, a good start was made in providing special training for the crews of the bombing force that was to grow to maturity in the summer of 1918.

Chapter 6

Strategic Plans and Operations, April to November 1918

A new and important phase in the history of British air operations began with the establishment of the second Air Council. The appointments of Sir William Weir as Secretary of State and Major-General F.H. Sykes as Chief of the Air Staff gave a new direction to strategic air thought, for both were convinced that the end of the war could be hastened by the systematic bombardment of German war industry. Sir William Weir, a Scottish engineer who possessed a wide knowledge of air problems, had been co-opted as a member of the Cowdray Air Board with responsibility for air equipment and supply. Soon after his appointment to the Board he had expressed himself strongly in favour of a long-range bombing campaign against Germany and had succeeded in gaining Lord Cowdray's support for this idea.[1]

> His ambition [wrote Andrew Boyle, in his biography of Trenchard] was to build bombers by the hundred to carry the war into Germany, for Weir regarded long-range aircraft potentially more devastating in their direct impact on the enemy's economy than the U-boat would prove on that of the British.[2]

General Sykes, on the other hand, had derived his conviction of the importance of strategic bombing from actual experience in the field. During his command of the air forces in the Eastern Mediterranean, he had directed long-range bombing attacks against the Berlin-Constantinople railway line along which munitions were transported to the Turks. Though he could achieve only limited success with the small forces at his disposal, he was impressed by a consideration of the injury that might be inflicted upon an enemy by large-scale attacks against the sources from which he derived his war material.[3]

The new Air Staff did not however underrate the difficult task which lay ahead. They were keenly aware of the fact that if strategic bombing was to make a contribution to the winning of the war, British policy would have to be reshaped at the highest level. This was the only way to secure the necessary priority for the bomber force.

This point was made with some feeling by Lieutenant-Colonel R.C.M. Pink, who was head of the section responsible for planning the independent bombing operations. In a memorandum to the Deputy Chief of the Air Staff, Colonel Pink expressed the fear that if a half-hearted attitude was adopted towards the campaign the only result would be 'another anaemic operation on the lines of the late No. 3 Wing, R.N.A.S., or the present business at Ochey'. The first step was to decide whether or not a bombing offensive was essential to the winning of the war. If the decision was in the affirmative, all available resources should be devoted to it; if not, it should be left entirely alone. An all-out effort was the only way to succeed in the bombing, and this, Colonel Pink believed, could only be achieved if the allocation of aircraft to the Navy and the Army was cut down to a minimum and the number of defence flights in England considerably reduced.[4]

One of the first steps towards the formulation of a bombing plan was the creation of a committee whose function was to consider the best means of implementing the policies decided by the Air Council. This committee, which was called the Strategic Council, consisted of four permanent members, the Chief of the Air Staff, the Deputy Chief of the Air Staff, the Director of Flying Operations and the Controller of the Technical Department. In addition, the Deputy Master General of Personnel, the Director of

Training and the Director of Air Organization were nominated as permanent advisers, but the Council also had the power to call before them any specialist officer whose advice they might need. The fact that the Chief of the Air Staff and his deputy were members both of the Air Council and the Strategic Council ensured a close liaison between the two bodies and obviated the risk of divided authority.

Briefly, the functions of the Strategic Council were to formulate plans for carrying out the policy decided upon by the Air Council, and upon obtaining the Air Council's approval of the plans, to carry them into effect. The air staff paper describing the functions of the Strategic Council gave an example of how this arrangement would operate.

> The Air Council might lay down the policy of bombing a German Key Industry; the Strategic Council would settle what number of bombs were necessary to obliterate any particular factory, the force necessary to obtain this number of direct hits and hence the order in which such factories should be destroyed, having regard to the force available at the time, and with what number of machines, and what system, this should be carried out.

One obvious advantage of this method of approach was that by maintaining a close liaison with the specialist branches the Strategic Council would be able to base its planning on a realistic assessment of what was possible in terms of the resources available. The Strategic Council would also be in a position to indicate to the specialists the likely requirements for the future, and this would ensure that action was taken in good time. For example, it might be necessary to set up a system of D/F stations to provide a navigational aid for aircraft operating over Germany. Or again, raids planned against a certain type of industry might require that a special bomb be designed and developed to produce the greatest effect against the types of buildings to be attacked.[5]

The first meeting of the Strategic Council was held on 22nd April 1918, and though the proceedings on this occasion do not seem to have been based on a prepared agenda, a list of suitable topics for discussion, drawn up by the Controller of the Technical Department, was distributed to the members. The most significant feature of the list was that it revealed a keen awareness of the technical nature of many of the problems involved in long-range bombing. The list comprised ten subjects, and it is interesting to note the three which were deemed to be of the highest importance. In order of priority, these were, first, the difficulties of navigation over long distances and the improvements in training techniques and equipment needed to overcome them; second, the possibility of using stabilized bombsights as standard equipment on all long-range bombers, and third, the necessity for improving the meteorological services, especially for providing information concerning the speed and direction of winds above the ground.[6]

The first meeting of the Strategic Council was spent in discussing various schemes that might be adopted to put into effect the Air Council's strategic policy. A plan was agreed in outline, and the Director of Flying Operations, Brigadier-General P.R.C. Groves, was asked to submit a paper dealing with the main factors involved in an air offensive. The paper, which completed two days later, was prepared by Lord Tiverton who was now a major in the Royal Air Force and the officer responsible for drawing up plans for the strategic bomber force.

The paper dealt mainly with the action that should be taken as a matter of urgency. The first priority, it was stressed, should be given to the compilation of data relating to the various aspects of bombing. Until this was done, it would not be possible either to estimate the size of force required or to devise the most effective operational tactics.

There were three main areas in which greater knowledge was required. First, more accurate information should be obtained concerning mean bombing errors, having due regard to certain factors – the new stabilized bomb-sight, for instance – which might affect them. Secondly, it was necessary to decide whether the D.H.4 or the Vimy type of aircraft would be the more efficient day-bomber. This decision was of the utmost importance in view of the large numbers of aircraft which would have to be used in daylight attacks to carry out the policy of 'obliterating' the major war factories. Finally, there was the problem of finding the best type of bomb for use against each type of building construction. For example, a five storey building such as the Bosch magneto works might best be attacked by bombs of 230 lb. or over, whereas a larger number of 112 lb. bombs might prove more effective against a single-storey building like the Mercedes engine works. But this was merely informed guesswork, for virtually no experiments on actual buildings had been carried out in France or in England. It was therefore suggested that a firm engaged in the demolition of buildings shattered in the air raids on London should be approached for information concerning the effect of various types of bombs.[7]

The fulfilment of the Air Staff's plans rested largely on the rapid expansion of the bomber force which in February 1918 had been raised in status, to become the 8th Brigade. But the improvement in aircraft production which it was hoped would be achieved by the spring of 1918 was not realized. At the end of April, when the first phase of the expansion programme should have been completed, increasing the strength of the force by three squadrons, no reinforcements had been received. Apart from the fact that the predicted increase in aircraft production was based on unrealistic thinking, the disappointing output for 1918 can in part be attributed to more specific reasons. The most important one was the failure of several aero-engines which the Air Board had approved for mass production.[8] Of these failures the most serious one was that of the B.H.P. (Beardmore-Halford-Pullinger) which was intended to be the main power unit for the D.H.4 bomber.[9]

Ironically, the firm which produced the most successful British aero-engines of the war, the Rolls-Royce Company (one of many

Photographs from the Report of the Bombing Commission on the Air Raids
on Germany.
(*Photo: Public Record Office*).

Photographs from the Report of the Bombing Commission on the Air Raids on
Germany.
(*Photo: Public Record Office*).

firms introduced by the Admiralty into this field of manufacture) was consistently thwarted by the Air Board in its attempts to improve and extend the output of engines.[10] Indeed, had it not been for large deliveries of Hispano-Suiza engines from France there would have been a serious shortage of engines in Britain by the beginning of 1918. These formed part of an order for 8,000 engines which the Admiralty, in spite of Lord Curzon's opposition, had persuaded the Air Board to place at the end of 1916. Lord Curzon based his opposition to the proposal on his belief that the war would be over before the engines were delivered late in 1917 or early in 1918.[11]

Another blow to the hopes of an early increase in the striking power of the bomber force was the poor performance of the D.H.9 which was intended to replace the D.H.4 as the standard day bomber in 1918. The decision to adopt the D.H.9, which was in fact a modified version of the D.H.4, was taken in July 1917 by the Air Board, who were led to believe that the new aircraft would have a better all-round performance than its predecessor.[12] But in November 1917 Trenchard wrote to Major-General J.M. Salmond, at that time Director-General of Military Aeronautics, saying that he had been informed unofficially by Mr Geoffrey de Havilland that the D.H.9 would be inferior in performance to the D.H.4 powered by the 275 horse-power Rolls-Royce engine.[13]

In a report dated 26th November 1917, Trenchard had this to say of the new aircraft:

It appears that they will not be able to fly in formation at 15,000 feet carrying a full load of bombs, and that they only carry enough petrol to reach the nearest German towns, and then only at a lower height than is attained in the case of the De Havilland 4's.[14]

When the matter was raised with the Air Board, Sir William Weir stated categorically that it was a case of having the D.H.9 with the B.H.P. engine, or of having nothing at all.[15]

M

In spite of these difficulties, the Air Council remained hopeful that the supply situation would soon improve, and in May 1918 steps were taken to create what had long been in the minds of the advocates of strategic bombing — an entirely independent bombing force. On the 13th of that month, the Air Council notified the War Cabinet that in their opinion:

> ... The time has arrived to constitute an independent force of the Royal Air Force for the purpose of carrying out bombing raids on Germany on a large scale. This will be organized as a separate command of the British Royal Air Force under Major-General H.M. Trenchard, who will work directly under the Air Ministry.[16]

The War Cabinet approved the policy and the Independent Force came into being. The creation of such a force, independent of his authority, was strongly resisted by General Foch, who had lately been appointed Allied Supreme Commander. He insisted, and won his point, that all air resources in France should be under his command and be available for use in support of the land campaign.[17] It is very doubtful whether the mere change of title was worth the ill-will it caused between the two allies, for when the Independent Force officially came into being, on 6th June 1918, it was no more than the 8th Brigade with the addition of two day squadrons.

Nevertheless, the Air Council, firm in their belief that the war would continue until at least the summer of 1919, looked to the future with confidence. This optimism was expressed in a memorandum which Sir William Weir wrote to the War Cabinet on 23rd May 1918. In it, he stated his belief that under the new air organization:

> ... a rapid development of aerial forces, devoted to the interruption of German industrial effort and kindred objects, might be achieved to such an extent as substantially to

contribute towards bringing about a definite demand for peace.[18]

This opinion was not shared by the staff officers responsible for the planning of strategic operations. They were concerned that the planning and preparation for the bombing offensive were not being pressed forward with sufficient energy, and their misgivings found expression in the memoranda written by Lord Tiverton at this time. In a paper dated 22nd May and addressed to the Chief of the Air Staff, Lord Tiverton pointed out that although many papers dealing with bombing policy had been written, no definite bombing plan for 1918 had been produced.

On 22nd April, when the Strategic Council first met, it would have been a fair assumption to count on 20 weeks during 1918 before the weather broke in the Rhine Valley. Four of these weeks have now gone and the matter is no further forward than when it was started.

He therefore proposed that as a matter of first priority 'a detailed plan should be drawn up forthwith for 1918, and by "forthwith" is meant the next twenty-four hours if the whole staff have to stop up all night to do it'. He believed that only by setting out in precise detail the targets we intended to attack could we hope to secure French co-operation in the offensive. Equally, he was convinced that immediate action should be taken to find new aerodrome accommodation, not only in the vicinity of the established aerodromes, but also in the region 'out of the Nancy salient where the ridge and furrow is much less . . .'. To this end, a team of experts should be despatched at once to carry out a systematic survey of the area bounded by Vitry-le-François, Chaumont, Belfort and the lines. If this were done, it would enable us:

. . . to answer the French objection which has obtained since

1916, that concentrated aerodromes will attract reprisal
bombing. A concrete proposal for the sites of aerodromes,
and the comparison between the numbers and concentration
on our side and the German side will soon show that no real
objection should be raised or could be sustained on this
ground.[19]

In another paper, dealing with various operational problems,
Lord Tiverton emphasized the importance of tackling at once the
problems which would inevitably appear when our French and
American allies made their contribution to the bombing offensive.
For example, an Anglo-French raid with Breguets and D.H.9's
would require careful preparation, since the normal formation
flying speed of the Breguet was some ten miles an hour slower
than that of the D.H.9. If, however, arrangements were to be made
to deal with such contingencies, it would be important to know in
advance the types of aircraft which, say, the French and
Americans intended to use for long-range operations. To minimize
such difficulties, it was essential that plans for joint operations
should first be discussed and approved by the Supreme War
Council, so that each nation participating in a scheme would know
exactly what preparations it was required to make. At the same
time, the process of decision making at this level must be
accelerated if the operational plans for 1918 were to be prepared
in time.

In the same paper, Lord Tiverton stressed the urgency of
obtaining the necessary data so that the error curve in bombing
could be calculated. The passage referring to this reads:

A good deal has been done with this already, and sufficient
data have been obtained to make a comparison between
various targets on the question of their vulnerability. It is,
however, thought of the utmost importance and urgency to
go beyond comparative figures and to attempt to get absolute
figures. Questions which come into this are so numerous that

it is difficult to divide them without getting a cross-section, but the number of bombs necessary, the effect of formation flying on the Error Curve, the time necessary to train the pilots in accurate bombing, the provision and maintenance in the field of accurate Gyro bomb sights, the actual choice of targets, the type of machine, are so intimately connected with this question and with one another that the whole matter must be treated as one large and complex question. It must of necessity take some time to solve and therefore cannot be taken up too soon.[20]

The bombing programme for 1918, for which Lord Tiverton had asked, was almost certainly never drawn up. Instead, the Air Staff concentrated on producing a plan, extending into 1919, which could be put into operation by a force of aircraft considerably smaller than that originally planned for. The results of this work were embodied in a number of papers written in June and July, but the essence of the revised scheme may be seen in two papers written by Lord Tiverton. The earlier of these papers, entitled 'Notes on Targets',[21] shows that the key industries chosen for attack were the chemical industry and the iron industry. It was considered that these two industries could be destroyed and that their destruction would affect the whole output of munitions.

Some eighty per cent of the whole chemical industry of Germany is concentrated in twelve works within raiding distance from the Nancy area. The contents are undoubtedly vulnerable and the works would be practically impossible to duplicate out of reach. The effect, therefore, of destroying these works would be to cut off the supply of high explosives, of mustard gas, and propellant powder.

The disruption of the iron industry was to be caused by systematic attacks on the German blast furnaces, eighty-three per cent of which were concentrated in forty-eight works, all within bombing distance. From the tactical point of view, the blast furnaces were considered to be admirable targets. They were most vulnerable to attack and were difficult to repair if damaged; they were clearly visible from the sky at night; and the majority of them were at very short distances from the bomber bases, so that they could be attacked when weather conditions prohibited operations at long range.

Consideration was given, too, to the industries manufacturing aero-engines and magnetos. These industries were regarded as objectives of first importance, but it was felt that attacks upon them should be postponed until the bomber force was sufficiently strong to obliterate the factories concerned in one or two raids.

> These works are, however, more easy to duplicate out of reach and therefore it would seem worthwhile holding back upon this until the strength is sufficient. They are concentrated in three works, the Bosch Magneto at Stuttgart, the Mercedes at Stuttgart and the Benz at Mannheim. If these were obliterated in two or three raids the whole of the German air programme would be put back for at least six months, probably more.

The second paper, entitled 'Paper on Targets within easy reach of Ochey',[22] contained descriptions and assessments of the relative importance of the targets in the chemical and iron industries, but its most significant feature was a statement of the functions of an independent bombing force and of the types of operations that such a force should not be required to undertake.

> The General policy which led to the formation of the Independent Force is the demobilization of the German Armies-in-the-Field by attacking the root industries which supply them with munitions.
>
> If it were possible a very much larger force than is at

present available should be allocated to carry out this policy. Unfortunately the exigencies in the Army and the Navy are such that only a comparatively weak force is available. The desired result can therefore only be obtained by employing the Independent Force strictly for the purpose which is in view and resolutely refusing its services in other directions however desirable they may appear in themselves.

The possible uses to which such Independent Force might be put besides the systematic destruction of German munitions are strategic reconnaissance and attacks upon railway centres, transport and enemy aerodromes. These however must be undertaken by the Air Units serving with the Armies-in-the-Field, otherwise with the very limited force available for independent operations no real progress will be made in the destruction of key industries.

Indeed, the question of attacking enemy aerodromes had recently been raised by Brigadier-General C.L.N. Newall, commander of the 8th Brigade. In a paper entitled 'The Scientific and Methodical Attack of Vital Industries',[23] he emphasized the importance of taking offensive action against enemy fighting and bombing squadrons which might be used against the bomber force. General Newall believed that if the Germans were allowed to gain the initiative in attacking our aerodromes the air offensive would be conducted under a severe handicap.

It is therefore essential that we should at once decide on a vigorous policy of attack on the enemy's aerodromes. At the moment the enemy has no bombing units operating in Lorraine, but no doubt they will appear shortly. We have numerical superiority, and can take the initiative when we choose to do so. Having once gained the upper hand we should have no difficulty in maintaining it. The enemy's bombing units can hinder both our night and day operations, whereas fighting machines can only effectively hinder day operations. We should therefore commence by a vigorous and concentrated attack on his bombing units, immediately they reappear in Lorraine, and having dealt with these we should then act similarly against his fighting machines.

The Air Staff reacted predictably to this suggestion. They had no hesitation in supporting the policy but were concerned as to how it could be carried out. Lord Tiverton raised this point in the comments he wrote for the Director of Flying Operations.

This raises at once the question as to whether the French Army-in-the-Field will be sufficient to undertake this work, or as to whether the Independent Force will have to do so. There is the greatest possible danger in this latter course of allowing the offensive to degenerate into a 'I bomb you and you bomb me' programme.[24]

Meanwhile Lord Tiverton was progressing with his research into problems concerning tactics and training. He was, however, conscious that the results he obtained would have been more accurate if he had possessed certain technical information which it was within the resources of the Air Ministry to supply.

In a memorandum addressed to the Director of Flying Operations, Lord Tiverton pointed out that he and Major Wimperis had arrived at theoretical estimates of the results to be obtained by bombing various targets, but that they lacked certain vital data with which to check the accuracy of their calculations. First, it was essential to have reliable figures concerning the percentage of bombs that might be expected to strike a particular type of target under given conditions. In order to obtain this information, Lord Tiverton suggested that full-size outlines of important German factories, such as the Badische Anilin und Soda Fabrik at Mannheim and the Bosch Magneto works at Stuttgart, should be marked out on Salisbury Plain and mock day and night attacks made against them. It would be important to simulate the conditions of an actual attack. For example, each target should be so orientated that pilots approached it on the same compass course as they would steer for the real target. Again, flares and searchlights could be positioned near the targets to reproduce the conditions of a night raid.

> The pilots [wrote Lord Tiverton] could use the one pound pilot bomb designed by Major Wimperis which gives in fact the same trajectory as the bombs which they will use. They will, by dropping these, of which they can carry an enormous quantity, not only be learning their targets and their method of attack, but also instruct the F.O. Directorate as to what results may be expected, and the Technical Directorate as to the defects which they find in their instruments.

Next in importance was to discover which types of bombs were most suitable for the various targets. Lord Tiverton suggested that several small committees of experts, under the Director of Aircraft Armament, should be set up to recommend the best types of bombs for use against chemical plants, factories manufacturing electrical components, and iron and steel works. This, he believed, would be the most efficient way of determining the number and types of bombs required to destroy any particular factory. Finally, he raised the point of what might be called the 'scientific method' of training pilots in target recognition.

> If long distance bombing is to be carried out effectively, the pilots must know their targets backwards. They should eat with them, sleep with them and dream of them and be able to make a rough sketch of any one of them out of their head. The only way that one can see in practice of doing this is to have models made which are to be put in the mess and which they constantly see.[25]

It is clear that Lord Tiverton's reason for attaching such

importance to this type of training was to reduce to a minimum the effort that was wasted by the failure of aircraft to locate their targets. If this suggestion concerning target recognition is considered in conjunction with his views that pilots should become thoroughly familiar with the area over which they must fly to reach their targets, it may reasonably be supposed that Lord Tiverton envisaged training pilots to navigate to and locate their targets in much the same way as they would be trained to operate, say, a machine-gun. That is to say, he wished to introduce as much 'drill' as possible into their training in navigation and target recognition in order to eliminate as far as possible the element of human error. In view of the many prominent landmarks in the operational area of the bomber force and of the relatively small number of factories which had been selected for attack, it is not improbable that he was thinking along these lines.

Hopes of positive action against Germany during 1918 were briefly encouraged by the apparently good progress made towards the establishment of a group of the Independent Force in East Anglia.[26] The decision, taken in May 1918, to set up this home-based group was a direct result of the production of the Handley Page V-1500, a new four-engined bomber which was expected to be capable of reaching many important German targets, including Berlin, from bases in England. Unfortunately, the first aircraft produced was wrecked in a crash in June, and it was not until October that the second aircraft was ready for flying trials.

Nevertheless, arrangements to form No. 27 Group at Bircham Newton, in Norfolk, had been pressed forward, and in September the first squadron, No. 166, began to mobilize.[27] Although the idea of bombing such German cities as Hamburg and Berlin, which had hitherto been well out of aircraft range, had its appeal even in official circles, the primary function of the new force was to be precisely the same as that of the Independent Force in France, namely, to destroy the German munition industry.

With this consideration clearly in mind, Lieutenant-Colonel R.H. Mulock, the Commander of No. 27 Group, decided that the industrial area of Westphalia offered the most promising targets for his bombers. He therefore requested the Air Ministry to suggest a method and plan of attack against this group of targets. The paper which was prepared in response to his request was the work of Lord Tiverton who agreed with Colonel Mulock's view of the importance of this industrial region.

All the trade experts are of the opinion first, that the Westphalian Group is the key group of the whole of the German munition production, and secondly that if the Group were thoroughly crippled Germany would not be able to carry on the war.

Even in the relatively restricted area with which he proposed to deal – the triangle defined by Duisburg, Dortmund and Cologne – Lord Tiverton realized there were so many desirable targets as to make a definite choice of objectives far from easy. Nevertheless, he thought it was vital to maintain the principle of concentration of effort and not to allow the campaign to degenerate into one of indiscriminate bombing. In his view, the bombing should be restricted to the six major steel producing plants which lay in the large conurbation which comprised Beeck, Ruhrort, Oberhausen, Meiderich, Mülheim, Rheinhausen and Duisburg. Not only did these plants make a large contribution to Germany's output of steel, but, because of their proximity to the Rhine, they were easy targets to locate compared, say, with the Krupp Works at Essen or the Tudor Accumulator Works at Hagen. Indeed, the two most important steel works, the Phoenix and the Rheinische Stahlwerke, both at Ruhrort, which was especially easy to find, virtually formed one target. After dealing with the claims of other possible targets, Lord Tiverton summed up by suggesting that the attacks should be directed exclusively against the steel targets until the six main works were destroyed or until the anti-aircraft defences became too strong to allow the offensive to be carried on without prohibitive losses.[28]

As the summer months passed it became increasingly obvious that the strategic offensive was no nearer realization than it had been when the second Air Council was formed. The expansion programme had fallen seriously behind schedule and the specialized training required by the crews in navigation, target identification and bomb-dropping had hardly begun. And almost equally dispiriting for the Air Staff was the knowledge that even the puny force that did exist was used largely against tactical objectives. Early in August Lord Tiverton recorded his thoughts on this subject for the Director of Flying Operations.

In April 1918 there came into being a new staff who were essentially associated with one definite policy, namely the intensive bombardment of Germany. The policy was defined as being the systematic obliteration (afterwards modified to 'dislocation') of the German industrial and munition works. . . . A systematic choice of key industries was begun upon paper and the chemical targets definitely chosen for priority. In fact the I.F. [Independent Force] have not systematically attacked them, or even attempted to do so. No systematic use has been made of the right type of bomb so that both the Technical Department and the technical officers of the Independent Force are in despair. Although models of all targets have been offered by the War Trades Intelligence, no intensive training in knowledge of such targets has been undertaken. In fact, therefore, nothing has been done to carry out the promised policy more than would have been done in any case. The policy put forward in April as the essential policy of the new staff has not in fact been carried out in any way. The very opposite policy has persistently been carried out with all the material available.

Lord Tiverton was also concerned that in other ways the operational policy laid down by the Air Ministry was ignored. He cited two examples. The first one concerned the decision

... that certain targets could not be bombed until sufficient strength was collected to obliterate them. For instance, the Bosch magneto works at Stuttgart; in fact these works have been raided and even the miserably small amount of aeroplanes which visited Stuttgart were not all employed against this works. It is an easy works for the Germans to duplicate out of range, and doubtless they will now do so without any material damage having been done. This was not done fortuitously as the G.O.C.I.F. made it one of the main objects of his July programme.

The second example concerned the question of target intelligence.

It has often been pointed out, that the pilots must be trained to know their targets, and yet on August 8th a raid was solemnly reported as having taken place on the Rombach explosive works. A.I.l.b. [A branch of Air Intelligence in the Air Ministry] say that they have no knowledge of any such works. Either some knowledge is in the possession of the I.F. which ought to be in the possession of the Intelligence, or the Intelligence of the I.F. is wholly wrong, or the pilots cannot have known what target they really were attacking, in which latter case it would be impossible for any pilot to pick out the vital spot in the particular works.[29]

This and other papers written by Lord Tiverton provided the Director of Flying Operations, Brigadier-General P.R.C. Groves, both with arguments and statistics for a strong protest to the Chief of the Air Staff. This took the form of a memorandum, written early in September, in which he sought to show that the policy approved for the employment of the Independent Force was not in fact being carried out. In support of this contention he provided details of the main types of targets against which the Force had been used during June, July and August of 1918.

The percentage of attacks carried out on Chemical Factories have dropped from 14% in June, to 9.5% in July, and to 8% in August. Similarly attacks on Steel and Iron Works show a decrease of from 13.3% in June, to 9% in July, and to 7% in August. An examination of the figures shows that this decrease has been caused by an increased activity against hostile aerodromes, the number of attacks rising from 13.3% in June to 49.5% in August.

Although he agreed that the commander of the Force must be the best judge of what action was necessary against enemy air bases, General Groves was convinced that too much effort had been directed against railway targets.

The percentages of attacks on railway establishments were 55% in June, 46% in July and 31% in August. It is submitted that this percentage, although decreasing, is still too high, and that it should be still further decreased and effort directed more against chemical works and steel factories.[30]

The Chief of the Air Staff supported General Groves's contention that the bombing operations should be made to conform with the Air Ministry plan, but it seems that he could do nothing to bring this about. Reasons to explain this failure are not difficult to find. In the first place, the Independent Force was not in any sense of the word independent. It continued to function only so long as its commander retained the goodwill of the French, and this good will was purchased at the price of making the bombing squadrons available for tactical support when required by the French army commanders. Secondly, the officer appointed to command the Independent Force was strongly opposed to strategic bombing and had no qualms about using his squadrons on tactical operations. Major-General M.M. Patrick, commander of the American Air Service in France, recorded Trenchard's opinion of the strategic operations.

General Trenchard told me that he had fought for several years against this independent show, but that it had been forced upon him.[31]

It was now clear that the original bombing plan was too ambitious and would have to be drastically revised. Early in October Lord Tiverton produced the outline of a programme which he thought could be fulfilled by September 1919. He suggested that attacks should be confined to a selected number of targets in the chemical and steel industries. He proposed five chemical plants and twelve steel works which he believed could be destroyed during the following year.[32] This was the last strategic plan to be considered by the Air Staff before the end of the war. When hostilities came unexpectedly to an end, on 11th November, all that remained to be done was for Lord Tiverton to write a brief history of long-distance bombing operations for the War Cabinet.[33]

* * *

The 8th Brigade began its operations as part of the Royal Air Force[34] with an effective strength of one day squadron. At the end of March, General de Castelnau, Commander of the French Eastern Group of Armies, requested that the two night squadrons should be placed temporarily under his command for the purpose of attacking railway communications in the Châlons-sur-Marne sector where a German offensive seemed imminent. On 1st April, Nos. 100 and 216 squadrons were transferred to an aerodrome at Villeseneux, near Rheims, where they remained until 9th May. During the period of their attachment to the French air service, the two squadrons were prevented by bad weather conditions from operating on more than six nights, when their targets included stations and sidings at Juniville, Amagne-Lucqy and Asfeld. Meanwhile No. 55 Squadron, from its base near Nancy, had attacked railways at Luxembourg, Metz-Sablon and Thionville, so that the whole effort of the force during April and early May was directed against railway objectives.

For the remainder of May, too, railways were the most frequent targets, but two operations against long-distance objectives in Germany were also achieved. On 18th May, six D.H.4's of No. 55 Squadron made the first daylight attack on Cologne since the naval raid on the city in October 1914. The approach of the raiders was not notified to the authorities in the city, and as a result casualties were high, forty people being killed and more than twice as many injured. Material damage was inconsiderable but the morale of the civilian population was severely shaken. As they were leaving the target, the D.H.4's were engaged by two formations of enemy aircraft, and in the fight which ensued at least one enemy machine was destroyed.

> There were reactions to this raid [wrote the Official Historian] similar to those which had followed the more important German attacks on England. Questions were asked in the Reichstag, and anxiety spread to all the Rhineland towns. It is significant also that after this first daylight attack in force on Cologne, it was urged in many responsible quarters in Germany that steps should be taken by the German Government to agree with the Allies to abandon or limit bombing attacks from the air.[35]

The second raid was made by Handley Pages of No. 216 Squadron against the Badische chemical plant at Mannheim, on the night of 21st/22nd May. Direct hits were scored on the section of the works at Oppau, and the damage which resulted from a fractured gas main closed the factory for two days. This was the only occasion during the war when production at the Oppau section of the works was halted by air action.

When operations opened in June, the force had received two more day squadrons, Nos. 99 and 104, equipped with D.H.9's. Significantly, both squadrons made their first raids against the Metz-Sablon railway triangles; for the number of attacks against railway objectives was still at a high level, and in June amounted to no less than 55% of all operations. In both June and July the presence of thick clouds over the Rhine valley frequently prevented operations against the more distant targets. During the latter month, however, attacks were possible against Mannheim, Stuttgart and Coblenz. In July, too, opposition from enemy fighting machines became more intense, and fifteen bombers were lost in air combat.

The heaviest loss in a single encounter was sustained by the D.H.9's of No. 99 Squadron on 31st July. As had been predicted, the D.H.9 powered by the 200 horse-power B.H.P. engine was totally inadequate for long-range daylight operations.[36] Nine aircraft of that squadron crossed the lines to bomb Mainz, but when the formation reached the vicinity of Saarbrücken it was attacked by a large number of German fighters. Considering that it would be impossible to reach Mainz in the face of such powerful opposition, the formation leader decided to attack Saarbrücken instead. He therefore altered course, but before the objective was reached four bombers had been shot down. The remaining five aircraft bombed the railway at Saarbrücken, but on the return flight the enemy fighters continued their attacks and three more bombers were shot down. As a result of this action, No. 99 Squadron was unable to resume normal operations for almost a month, for the replacement pilots first had to be trained to fly together in formation.

During the month of August the strength of the Independent Force was increased by four squadrons. These were three squadrons of Handley Pages, Nos. 97, 115 and 215, and one squadron of D.H.9a's, No. 110. In addition, the F.E.2b's of No. 100 Squadron were gradually replaced by Handley Pages, and the re-equipment was completed early in September. Weather conditions in August were more favourable for long-distance flights, and among the German cities attacked were Düren, Frankfurt, Darmstadt, Cologne and Mannheim. The attack on Frankfurt, on 12th August, was the first one against that city by British aircraft. It caused panic throughout the city for several

N

days and evoked from the citizens stern criticism of the Government and the military authorities. Twelve D.H.4's of No. 55 Squadron were engaged in the operation, and although they were subjected to attacks by enemy fighters both on the outward and return flights, all the bombers returned safely, having destroyed two enemy aircraft.

Another raid which is worthy of mention was made by two Handley Pages of No. 215 Squadron against the Badische chemical works at Mannheim, on the night of 25th/26th August. Having located their target, the two pilots came down below five hundred feet to drop their bombs, the majority of which fell on the factory.

> Germans in and near the works, [wrote the Official Historian] looked upon this attack as particularly daring, and their evidence was that the bombers only narrowly missed the tall factory chimneys. Many of the bombs, possibly as a result of the low height from which they were dropped, failed to explode, but four which penetrated one of the buildings burst among a freezing plant which could not be brought into action again for twelve days.[37]

But if the weight of the bombing attacks was increasing, so was the resistance mounted by the German fighting formations, and during August twenty-one British aircraft were lost in the air fighting. The response of the commander of the Independent Force was to increase the number of attacks against enemy bases, and in August the effort against aerodromes amounted to nearly 50% of the operations carried out by the bombing squadrons.

In September, weather conditions deteriorated and high winds and low cloud were prevalent over a wide area. In consequence, no operations were possible on nineteen days and eighteen nights. Nevertheless, attacks were made against the German cities of Frankfurt, Mannheim, Cologne and Mainz, among others. By this time, the enemy night defences had become more effective, and the night bombers, which had hitherto operated almost with impunity, began to encounter stiff opposition from the ground defences. On the night of 16th/17th September, seven Handley Pages from the various squadrons were lost, and it is probable that six of them were destroyed by anti-aircraft gunfire. It is recorded that in the area over which the Handley Pages were operating the Germans fired 16,063 anti-aircraft shells and brought into action 173 searchlights.[38]

On two occasions in the month, Marshal Foch made formal requests for the assistance of the Independent Force in offensives planned by the French and American armies. This assistance was readily given, and on the first occasion, the American attack on the St. Mihiel Salient, raids were carried out on railways and aerodromes, between the 12th and 17th September. During this period the weight of bombs dropped was sixty-one tons, of which about half was directed against the Metz-Sablon railway triangle. The second request, which was made on 23rd September, was for support for an offensive by French and American forces in the Verdun area. The bombing attacks, which again were chiefly against railway targets, began on 26th September and were continued throughout the night of 26th/27th, after which unfavourable weather conditions prevented further operations during the few remaining days of the month.

Low cloud and poor visibility were common features of the weather during October, and few long-distance raids were attempted. As in September, Marshal Foch requested the assistance of the British bombing squadrons, this time to aid the American and French armies in their offensive between Rheims and Verdun. Something approaching sixty tons of bombs were dropped on the railway centres at Metz-Sablon, Mézières and Thionville. One raid, however, which is worthy of mention was made by a number of Handley Pages against Kaiserslautern on the night of 21st/22nd October. On that occasion, three of the Handley Pages each carried one of the new 1,650 lb. bombs, and one of these bombs scored a direct hit on a small arms factory, a building of three storeys, and demolished it completely.

During the remaining days of the war, weather conditions were generally unfavourable for long-distance flights, the chief targets up to 11th November being railways and aerodromes at short range.

Soon after the end of hostilities the Air Ministry despatched a small commission to Germany to assess the effects of the British air attacks carried out during 1918. The members of the commission, who visited the most important towns and cities which had suffered air raids, questioned local officials and examined such documents and records as were still at hand. Their findings were embodied in an official document dated January 1920.[39]

The evidence gathered by the commission shows beyond doubt that the injury inflicted upon the enemy was out of all proportion to the size of the bomber force involved It is true that material damage caused by bombing was relatively small, but the constant raids depressed the morale of the civilian population, who by 1918 were war-weary and dis-spirited, and caused a considerable loss of industrial production. In addition, the Germans were compelled to construct a widespread air defence system which absorbed much valuable war material.[40]

There is abundant evidence of the effect of the bombing on civilian morale. For example, the efficiency of the operatives in the Volklingen, Burbach and Hagendingen steel works declined seriously as a result of the frequent air raid alerts during the summer and autumn of 1918.[41] Again, numerous letters which fell into British hands on the Western Front testified to the distress suffered by those who were subjected to the bombing.

An eye-witness of the British raid on Coblenz on 12th March concluded an account of the attack with the following words:

We have lived through terrible hours in the last day. Oh, my God, if only this misery was at an end, this useless murder of men.[42]

Another example was written by an inhabitant of Stuttgart, and dated 19th September.

> Martha has already written telling you what a terror aeroplanes have been to us lately. Before they come I always say to myself that I will not be afraid, but when they get here I become almost paralysed and then go into a state of collapse. This shows that these raids weaken and exhaust us. It is dreadful, everyone is terror stricken.[43]

As was the case in England during the Zeppelin raids, serious loss of industrial production was caused by the practice of sounding air-raid warnings over the whole area in which hostile aircraft were operating. Two examples of how output was reduced by air-raid alerts rather than by bombing may be quoted from the Official History.

> The Mannesmann works at Bous were bombed eight times between September 1916 and November 1918, and the damage was said to have been very small, estimated at a total of about £400. In the same period, however, the Mannesmann works received 301 air-raid alarms, as a result of which 454 working hours were lost, with a consequent drop in output, estimated by the managers at 9,440 tons. At the Volklingen works, in the same years, there were 327 alarms and a loss of output of 30,680 tons of steel.[44]

But perhaps the most telling effect of the air bombing was that it compelled the enemy to employ large numbers of aircraft, guns and searchlights, as well as the personnel to man them, to defend the threatened areas in Germany. In particular, the constantly increasing number of fighting units needed to combat the growing bombing offensive placed a great strain on German resources. It was estimated that in August 1918 there were on the Alsace, Lorraine and Verdun fronts a total of 90 enemy fighting aircraft

whose duties included the interception of hostile bombers. During
the next two months, 240 further fighting machines were brought
in to protect these fronts, so that by the end of the war a total of
330 first-class fighting aircraft had been assembled to oppose the
Independent Force which at its maximum strength numbered just
over 120 aircraft.[45]

It now remains to consider the tactics employed by the
squadrons of the Independent Force.[46] The tactics used by the
day bombers, the D.H.4's and D.H.9's, were in the main
determined by the need to evade the enemy air defences, and
especially the fighters. The bombers flew as high as they could
operate without loss of efficiency, in order to keep above the
effective range of the anti-aircraft guns, and to compel the fighters
to use up valuable time and fuel in reaching the necessary height
to engage. In addition, they maintained close formation so that
they could bring their combined fire-power to bear on attacking
fighters. Long experience had taught that several bombers flying in
organized formation were able to defend themselves successfully,
except when they were heavily outnumbered. Usually a group of
five or six bombers flew in a V formation, and when a larger
number of aircraft were operating, two or more V formations were
adopted. As soon as an attack was imminent, the formations
closed together to give mutual support. During the last phase of
the bombing offensive, the Germans began to use large formations
of fighters, commonly called 'circuses', to intercept the bombers,
and it was one of these formations that was responsible for the
destruction of seven D.H.9's of No. 99 Squadron.

Trenchard was much concerned by the growing power of the
enemy's fighter defences, and in a letter to the C.A.S. on 4th
August, he suggested that either two-seater fighters with extra fuel
capacity or bombers equipped as fighters should be used to escort
the bombers. The Flying Operations Directorate, however, advised
the C.A.S. that the provision of such escorts would impose a great
strain on our resources and suggested that the answer to the

problem lay 'in the adoption of larger formations or of groups of small formations so flying as to cover each other'.[47]

A serious operational weakness of the Force was the extent to which both day and night squadrons relied on the use of topographical maps for navigation. Map-reading was obviously an important element of navigation, but it should have been used in conjunction with other navigational techniques. These had been developed by the Admiralty, who in 1917 produced a number of instruments, among them the Course and Distance Indicator, the Drift Indicator and the Douglas Protractor, for use in air navigation. But few of these instruments were ever supplied to the squadrons of the Independent Force. It is true that navigation formed an important part of the courses provided by the schools of navigation and bomb-dropping, but such training was of little value if even the most elementary navigational instruments were lacking on the suadrons. The staff officers from No. 7 Training Group, pointed this out when they visited the Independent Force.

It may be confidently be stated, [they wrote in their report] that many of the faults attributed to training are in reality directly due to lack of proper equipment. For example, the observer who is equipped only with Maps, Paper and Pencil cannot be expected to detect with accuracy any alteration in the strength or direction of the wind.

The lack of essential navigational equipment would, however, have been less severely felt if reliable meteorological information had been available, but this was not the case. The Force did not possess its own meteorological facilities and it was generally acknowledged that the service provided by the organization known as 'Meteor' was quite inadequate. The forecast winds were often supplied many hours before an operation was due to begin and in some cases did not even apply to the height at which the aircraft were to fly. Nor had the crews proper facilities for checking the speed and direction of the wind when once they reached operational height. Although the high altitude drift sight could be used for wind-finding, this operation necessitated the aircraft being manoeuvred to fly up or down wind, followed by a 90 degree alteration of course – a procedure that was impossible when the bombers were flying in formation. Even if this had been feasible, it was, in practice, found impossible to take an accurate drift over 10,000 feet, and even below that height the lateral oscillation of the aircraft made the measurement of drift extremely difficult.

Lengthy experiments had been carried out at Orfordness to enable aircraft to navigate through and above cloud by flying on an accurate compass course.[48] Although a considerable degree of success had been attained during trials, this method of navigation could not be attempted by the squadrons of the Independent Force, again because of the lack of proper instruments. The only suitable compass for this work was the R.A.F. Mk. II, and neither this nor the Turn Indicator, which was essential for cloud flying, were available.

The standard bombsight on the day bombers was the high altitude drift, though the negative lens sight was used for actual bombing on the D.H.4's. The most common practice was to set the forecast wind on the sight before take-off; only very rarely was a check made on the wind during the flight. The bombers operated and dropped their bombs from the very highest altitude they could fly in ordered formation. At the end of the flight, the bombers attacked the target, either up or down wind, by the method known as 'flock' bombing; that is, all the aircraft in the formation dropped their bombs on a pre-arranged signal from the leader. The actual sighting on the target was done by the leader's observer only, while the pilots of the other aircraft released their bombs.

Quite different factors decided the tactics used at night. The night bombers operated singly, for the fear of collisions in the darkness was very strong. Enemy air defences presented few dangers and the height at which the aircraft flew – varying from a few hundred to 8,000 feet — was determined by weather conditions and the nature of the operation.

The standard sight on the Handley Pages was the high altitude drift with luminous scales. The sight was fitted to the nose of the aircraft and was operated from the front cockpit by the observer, who had an uninterrupted view both ahead and below. On the run-up to the target the bomb-aimer guided the pilot by means of hand signals, for, as in the day bombers, this was the only means of communication between pilot and observer. The wind used for bombing was invariably obtained from the meteorological service and was set on the sight before take-off.

The navigation used was of the simplest kind. The bombers flew on courses worked out in advance and checked their positions by map-reading. In conditions of good visibility, many objects on the ground could easily be identified from the heights at which the aircraft operated. On the return flight the bombers were able to establish their position by means of electric beacons situated near their aerodromes. These beacons, which flashed a letter in the morse code, were known as 'lighthouses'. The bombers were also able to make use of the signals which were transmitted from German aerodromes behind the lines. These consisted of a number of green flare shells, called by the British crews 'flaming onions', which were fired in a definite time sequence. These signals were navigational aids for enemy night-flying aircraft and were the German equivalent of the 'lighthouses'.

The tactics employed by the night bombers on their flights over enemy territory were such as to produce a depressing effect on morale, and how that was achieved is well described in the Official History.

The bombers did not attack in formation, but moved about singly, at irregular intervals of time, and they usually flew at low heights, making a noise that was full of menace. All over the area within range of the British bombers, people received the air-raid warning and had to take whatever precautionary measures had been ordered, perhaps dozens of times for every attack their particular town or works suffered. It was the 'alarms', more than the specific attacks, which led to idleness, temporary or prolonged, and therefore lowered output, and it was at night that it was difficult to keep alarms within reasonable relation to the possible danger.[49]

Reflections on the Air War

When the war came to an end all but a small number of the Royal Air Force squadrons in France were engaged in support of the land forces. After four years of war, Britain's powerful air service was still fulfilling the role for which the small force of military aircraft had been established before the war: that of an auxiliary of the British Army. The great potential of strategic bombing was still largely unexplored.

The majority of accounts of the air war are based on the assumption that, because of the nature of the warfare which developed on the Western Front, British air power was used to greatest effect in direct support of the land forces. This assumption that, because of the nature of the warfare which evidence to show that the Germans suffered more severely from the small-scale raids against their industrial cities than from the large-scale air offensives on the Western Front.

The truth is that the military air leaders, who controlled the greater part of Britain's air strength, were convinced that tactical support was the essential function of air power and strove to prevent the use of aircraft on strategic operations. They had no difficulty in gaining the support of the Air Board for their views and early in 1917 were able to secure from the Admiralty large quantities of air material which had been set aside for long-range bombing operations. As a result, the first British strategic bomber force – No. 3 Naval Wing – was disbanded, and the opportunity of co-operating with the French in an air offensive against Germany was irrevocably lost.

The Air Board continued to accept without question the operational policy of the Flying Corps and to support the insatiable demands for air resources for the military squadrons. Finally, in the summer of 1917, the British Government intervened and decreed the formation of a strategic bomber force. But it was already too late, and by the time the force was organized in the spring of 1918, the war was entering its final phase.

In order to understand why Britain's air strength was so completely committed to army support, it is essential to appreciate the extent to which Sir David Henderson was able to influence the direction of air policy both before and during the war. In 1912 he was a member of the sub-committee appointed by the Committee of Imperial Defence to draw up plans for the formation of a Flying Corps with a naval and military wing. Though the report of the sub-committee was issued under the names of all the committee members, it was in fact the work of four army officers, of whom only one, Henderson himself, was a member of the sub-committee. The report advocated the creation of an air service whose primary task, both on the naval and military side, would be reconnaissance. This was an astonishing proposal in view of the fact that in 1909 the Esher Committee had urged the Government to make preparations for defence against air attack and to explore the offensive potential of the flying machine. Equally surprising, the recommendations of the sub-committee were accepted without further consideration.

Thus, when the Military Wing of the R.F.C. came into existence, it was organized purely as an extension of the reconnaissance arm of the British Army. The most suitable type of aircraft for reconnaissance was considered to be one that was slow and stable; and with these characteristics in mind, the Royal Aircraft Factory began to produce the aircraft whose performances under war conditions proved to be hopelessly inadequate. Indeed, so convinced was Henderson that this estimate of the ideal aircraft was correct, that he issued an order prohibiting the Aircraft Factory from producing an aero-engine of more than 100 horse-power. Meanwhile, the Admiralty, taking an entirely different view of the use of air power in war, concentrated on developing the aeroplane as an instrument of the offensive. The Naval Wing experimented with aircraft fitted with machine-guns and carried out extensive trials in bomb-dropping; and at the outbreak of war had made considerable progress in preparing the service to undertake offensive duties. The Military Wing, on the other hand, had created a force of slow, unarmed aeroplanes, capable of operating over hostile territory only so long as anti-aircraft defences remained almost non-existent.

By the summer of 1915 the inadequacy of the military aircraft to perform the increasing range of army support duties was patent. In particular, tactical bombing, which was attempted on a considerable scale, brought heavy losses and little success to the squadrons which possessed neither the equipment nor the training for this work. Yet the aeronautical department of the War Office profited little from the experience of the first year of the war, and seems to have concentrated mainly on organizing the supply of even larger numbers of the aircraft types which had performed so badly in the opening phase of the war. Even when Henderson returned to the War Office as Director-General of Military Aeronautics there was no radical change in the situation.

In France, however, a new and important factor entered into the air war. After Henderson's departure, Trenchard, who assumed command of the R.F.C.-in-the-Field, at once put into practice his doctrine that aircraft, to be effective in war, must be used in the offensive. This involved putting aircraft into the air on every possible occasion and constantly carrying the air fighting into enemy territory. In conditions favourable to the British this policy might have been successful; but because of the general inferiority of British aircraft compared with those of the enemy, together with the fact that the air fighting on the Western Front favoured the defence, it resulted in heavy losses, with few compensating gains.

Nevertheless, Trenchard persisted with these tactics, and in

consequence was forced to make incessant demands for reinforcements in aircraft and men. This policy evoked more opposition
than is commonly supposed, and the views of those who spoke out
against it are nowhere more accurately and succinctly recorded
than in the Official History.

> It has been argued [wrote H.A. Jones] that the policy was ill
> conceived, or else that if it was sound in principle it was not
> applied with military wisdom. It has also been said that the
> air offensive was responsible for severe casualties, which led
> to the sending of reinforcements to France before they were
> adequately trained, with the result that they were offered as
> somewhat easy targets, so that the circle of heavy casualties
> and ill-trained reinforcements became a vicious one.[1]

The reinforcements which Trenchard so frequently demanded
were becoming increasingly difficult to provide, for the War Office
had planned neither for the production of aircraft nor for the
training of pilots and observers on the scale then required. The
most obvious way of easing the situation would have been to
suspend the 'offensive' policy in France. There was however a
more desirable alternative: to secure from the Admiralty air
material that was being assembled for an offensive against
Germany. Accordingly, Henderson asked the Air Board for a
ruling to the effect that the Flying Corps should have sole
responsibility for the conduct of air operations over land. His
object was to secure an increased share of the limited air material
for the military service. When this move did not succeed, he
enlisted the support of Haig and Trenchard in a protest against the
naval air policy. This intervention produced the desired effect. A
large amount of naval equipment was transferred to the Flying
Corps, and as a result the naval bombing wing at Luxeuil was
disbanded. By the spring of 1917 the War Office had considerably
strengthened the air forces under its control in the western
theatre. Then came a dramatic change in the pattern of events.

In May 1917 the Germans began to raid England with aircraft operating from Belgian airfields. After two daylight attacks on London, the Government, under severe pressure from public opinion, decided that retaliatory raids should be made against German cities. At the same time, the Cabinet appointed General Smuts to carry out an investigation into Britain's air policy and organization. Greatly impressed by the potential of long-range bombing carried out by large numbers of aircraft, General Smuts recommended the creation of a strategic bomber force, as part of an independent air force with its own staff to plan and direct the strategic air war. To a greater extent than is often appreciated, General Smuts based his recommendation on the expectation of a large surplus of aircraft in 1918. It was from this surplus that he intended the bomber force should be created. However, this estimate of a surplus was from the beginning a complete misreading of the situation. There was never any chance that it would materialize, and in consequence the air staff planning of 1918 was based on expectations which were impossible of fulfilment.

At this point it will be appropriate to consider in what respects the strategic policy developed in 1918 differed from the air force doctrine of the inter-war years which failed so badly when put to the test in the Second World War. Experience in the second war showed that the effects of bombing had been greatly overestimated, while the operational difficulties involved in long-range operations   navigation and bomb-aiming, for instance — had been seriously underestimated. These errors of judgement were made because the feasibility of operational policy was never subjected to scientific scrutiny. In the years between the wars it was assumed that a bomber could be flown to a distant target, both by night and day, by means of map-reading, and could hit a precise target from heights exceeding 15,000 feet. Yet no long-distance flights simulating war-time conditions were ever attempted, nor were valid bombing trials made at heights over 12,000 feet. Again, it was merely assumed that industrial targets could be destroyed by bombing, but nothing was known of the numbers or types of bombs that would be required for various kinds of factories.[2]

No such criticism could fairly be levelled against the Air Staff of 1918. In the first place, they knew from actual experience that the relatively short flights from French aerodromes to the German targets were operationally feasible. The day bombers were able to operate effectively in spite of enemy anti-aircraft defences, and the night bombers had no difficulty in finding their way in an area which contained many prominent features. This was the very reverse of the situation in the early years of the second war, when the day bombers could not survive against hostile fighters guided by radar, and the night bombers were seldom able to locate their targets after long flights over the blacked-out enemy countryside.

Secondly, the operational problems to which answers were urgently sought in 1918 were investigated by scientific methods. The officer responsible for initiating much of this work was Lord Tiverton, who based his investigations on techniques which were re-discovered and used with impressive results in the Second World War. Lord Tiverton was conscious of the need for accurate and up-to-date information on which to base his calculations and he constantly pressed for experiments and trials to fill the gaps in his knowledge. He was especially concerned to have reliable information on the factors affecting bomb-dropping so that he could calculate the effort required to destroy various kinds of targets. In this way, he could estimate the number of aeroplanes and the weight of bombs (revised from time to time as factors changed) that would be needed to fulfil a certain policy. There is of course no way of knowing how accurate these figures were, since the bombing campaign was never attempted, but the success of this method of solving operational problems in the Second World War suggests that the accuracy would have been high.[3]

Finally, in view of the exaggerated claims made for strategic bombing during the period between the wars, it is important to ask in what way these differed from the claims put forward for this type of bombing in 1918. The essential difference is that the claims made in 1918, that air bombing could be a decisive factor in achieving victory, was based on the scientific evaluation of the experience of nearly four years of war; whereas the claims of the inter-war years, that major nations might be made to sue for peace by the bombing of centres of population, was made during a period of peace which was marked by a revolution in aeronautics, the outcome of which no one could foresee. The question of numbers is important, too. The belief in strategic bombing held in the inter-war years — it was in fact more a faith than a policy — took no account of the size of the force required to produce the desired result, even assuming that this was attainable. The Air Staff of 1918, on the other hand recognized that large numbers of bombs, and therefore of bombers, would be needed to destroy the selected factories. They were under no illusions concerning the high percentage of bombs that would be wasted in attacks on precise targets. No one who examines the documents relating to this period can fail to be impressed by the estimates of the size of the force that was considered essential. For instance, in April 1918, Lord Tiverton's calculations of the effort required to destroy various types of factories indicated a bomber force of something over seven hundred aircraft. It is now obvious that a force of that size could not possibly have been assembled before the end of the war. But in the spring of 1918, with the end of the war seemingly as distant as ever, the task of creating such a force seemed far from impossible. By the spring of 1919, the production of the Handley Page V-1500 and the Vickers Vimy was expected to be well advance, while a substantial contribution to the bomber force was expected from the Americans.

The evidence presented in this study suggest two conclusions: first, that British air power was not used to the greatest effect in the tactical role, and secondly, that greater injury could have been inflicted upon Germany by a large-scale offensive against her war industry. So long as the air fighting was confirmed to the area of the front the Germans, though numerically weaker in aircraft, were able to hold their own without undue difficulty; but if their

o

industrial centres had been subjected to attack, they would have been compelled to fight a type of air war for which they were quite unprepared. This is not to imply that the war could have been won by strategic bombing, or that the greater part of Britain's air strength should have been devoted to this work: it is merely to suggest that a strategic bomber force, operating in conjunction with the French bomber groups, should have been a permanent formation in the British air force.

The key to an understanding of the use of air power on the Western Front is to be found in Trenchard's policy of the offensive. The object of this policy was to force the Germans on the defensive by carrying the air war into their territory. In practical terms, this meant operating as often as possible, and with all available strength, on the German side of the lines. Unfortunately, the circumstances were such that these tactics could only be pursued by placing the British squadrons at a severe disadvantage. First, since much of the air fighting took place over enemy-held territory, forced landings by British aircraft invariably resulted in the loss of both pilots and aircraft. Secondly, owing to the direction of the prevailing winds on the Western Front, British aircraft usually made the return flight to base in the face of the wind. This was a serious handicap to aircraft that were damaged or short of fuel. Thirdly, many of the standard British aircraft were of poor performance and suffered heavy losses in combat. Especially vulnerable were the slow reconnaissance aircraft, such as the B.E.2c's.

Trenchard never doubted that these tactics were successful in preventing the Germans from taking the initiative in the air, and in spite of the heavy casualties suffered by the military squadrons, he continued to press the offensive with unbending determination. However, it is certain that the Germans adopted a defensive policy by deliberate choice. They usually preferred to fight behind their own lines, and in the limited operational area at the Front these defensive tactics were pursued with complete success. Few hostile aircraft could cross the lines unobserved, and whenever allied aircraft appeared in strength an adequate number of fighting aircraft could quickly be assembled from the aerodromes which were thickly scattered over the area to the rear of the lines.

Further, since the operational area at the front was not their own territory, the Germans were able to concentrate on defending those targets which were of purely military value. It was of no embarrassment to them that large numbers of allied bombs fell on French towns and villages and damaged French property. But if the area behind their lines had been German soil, they would have been obliged, for obvious reasons, to provide a tighter defence system to prevent the incursions of allied aircraft.

Thus, the greater part of British air power was deployed in a theatre of war in which the scope for inflicting injury upon the Germans was extremely limited. The intention was that the sustained offensive would so weaken the German Air Force as to render it powerless to protect the German Army during the allied land offensives. So far was this policy from succeeding that during many crucial periods of the land battles the Germans actually gained the upper hand in the air. Indeed, the only possible justification for the offensive policy would have been found in the fact that the Germans suffered losses comparable to those of the British. But, in fact, this was not the case, as the Official Historian recorded.

> From a consideration of German official statistics supplied by the Reichsarchiv it would appear that the offensive which was relentlessly pursued in the air by the British air service was about four times more costly than the defensive policy adopted by the Germans.[4]

There was however a clear alternative to the policy which concentrated the whole of Britain's air strength on the Western Front where the advantages lay mainly with the Germans. This was the formation of a strategic bombing force to strike directly at Germany. If this had been done, the main air battle ground of the war might well have been transferred from the unprofitable region of France behind the enemy lines to the great industrial areas of Germany. For Germany's greatest weakness in a war which depended to an important degree on industrial output was that the bulk of her munitions of war were produced in the areas of Germany which lay within aeroplane range of French bases. The Germans enjoyed no such advantage in relation to the Allies, since most of the important industrial areas in Britain and France were too distant from the German aeroplane bases. Though the Zeppelins did in fact possess the necessary range, they were too few in number and too vulnerable to anti-aircraft defences to present a serious threat.

If the Allies had continued to develop the air offensive begun by the Admiralty and the French air service in 1916, they could have exploited a type of air warfare in which they enjoyed most of the advantages. Large-scale air attacks against the major industrial centres would not only have disrupted the production of war material, but would have faced the Germans with the almost impossible task of providing air defences for the threatened areas. The chief problems of defence were concerned with the provision of air material, and especially of fighting aircraft. Because of the large areas to be defended and the wide choice of targets offered to the bombers, two or three fighting aircraft were required in defence for every aircraft in the bomber force. Even the small-scale operations of No. 3 Naval Wing and, later, of the Independent Force showed clearly the pattern of strategic warfare. The Germans were compelled to maintain a large defensive force which contributed nothing to their striking power, whereas every operation carried out by the bombers disrupted production, and every bomb dropped on an industrial area destroyed enemy property and affected the morale of the workers.

Unfortunately, the Allies did not attempt to exploit a situation which was so advantageous to them, but chose to fight the type of air war which favoured the Germans. This was because the opinions which prevailed were those advocating the complete subordination of the air arm to the land forces. The turning point came when the British military air leaders were able to secure the disbandment of No. 3 Naval Wing, for the dispersal of the naval squadrons not only halted the naval operations but also brought the French bombing effort to an end. This then was the first, and the last, attempt made by the two allies to attack the enemy war industry. Thereafter, almost the whole of Britain's air power in the western theatre was committed to the air war over the trench-lines.

SOURCES

Sources

The source material for this study has been drawn almost entirely from the collection of documents relating to the Royal Naval Air Service, the Royal Flying Corps, and the Royal Air Force in the Public Record Office. In addition to the official records of the British air services, this collection contains important contemporary material relating to the development of naval and military aviation, collections of papers donated by private individuals, and many invaluable papers written by members of the Air Historical Branch during the inter-war years. The source material for the period up to 1918 is for the most part contained in the AIR 1 series. Reference to a specific document usually contains two parts, for example AIR1/122, 15/40/136. The first part indicates Box No. 122 of the AIR 1 series; the second part is the reference number of a file containing the document in question.

Apart from the documents in the Public Record Office, the papers of the 2nd Earl of Halsbury shed most light on the development of air strategic thought and practice during the First World War. Of considerable importance as a source of information are the various aviation journals, such as *Flight, The Aeroplane* and *Flying*. The papers of the 1st Viscount Weir were also consulted.

For the convenience of the reader, however, reference is made whenever possible to published works. Of these, the most important are the official history, *The War in the Air* by Sir Walter Raleigh and H.A. Jones, referred to in the notes by the abbreviation *W1A*, and *Documents Relating to the Naval Air Service, Volume 1 1908-1918*, edited by Captain S.W. Roskill, referred to as *NAS*. Of great value, too, are the introductory chapters of the first volume of *The Strategic Air Offensive against Germany 1939-1945*, by Sir Charles Webster and Noble Frankland.

Introduction

1.   For an essay on the nature of strategic air operations see *The Strategic Air Offensive against Germany 1939-1945*, by Webster and Frankland, Vol. I, Ch. 1.

2.   The story of this first period is the subject of Webster and Frankland op. cit.

3.   Webster and Frankland, op. cit., Ch. IV.

4.   For an expression of this view see Slessor: *The Central Blue*, pp. 366-7.

5.   The doctrine of the offensive is stated in an HQ RFC paper 'Future Policy in the Air', 22nd September 1916; W1A, Vol. II, Appendix IX, pp. 472-5.

For a highly critical view of this doctrine, see Groves: *Behind the Smoke Screen*, p. 123 foll.

6.   Boyle: *Trenchard*, pp. 204-5.

7.   AIR 1/30, 15/1/151.

8.   For the establishment of the first of these schools see AIR 1/122, 15/40/136.

9.   For a description of the aperiodic compass see Hughes: *History of Air Navigation*, pp. 100-2.

10.   The air navigational instruments in use in September 1918 are described in AIR 1/1084, 204/5/1710.

11.   See naval staff paper concerning the progress in air D/F W/T up to the end of 1917, AIR 2/38.

12.   For the use of D/F W/T on the Belgian coast, see AIR 1/634, 17/122/106.

13.   See CAS minute, 13th June 1918, regarding D/F W/T facilities, AIR 2/76.

14.   The various bombsights used in the war are briefly described in an air staff paper, 'Short Notes on the Evolution and Theory of Bomb Sights', 8th February 1921, AIR 1/674, 21/6/77.

15.   See report on the trials of this bombsight, 11th December 1917, AIR 2/38.

16.   For details of this aircraft and how it was to be operated see AIR 1/461, 15/312/103 and AIR 1/1978, 204/273/68.

17.   *WIA*, Vol. II, pp. 451-3; Vol. VI, 118-22.

Chapter 1

1.   *WIA*, Vol. III, p. 69.

2.   See article in *Flight*, No. 50, p. 796, 11th December 1909.

3.   Report of the Esher Committee, 28th January 1909, AIR 1/2100, 207/28/1.

4.   Report of the speech in *The Times*, 26th April 1909, p. 19.

5.   House of Commons, 2nd August 1909, Parliamentary Debates, Vol. VIII 1909, Cols. 1606-1610.

6.   The pamphlet outlining the aims of the League is to be found in AIR 1/653, 17/122/490.

7.   Letter from the League to the Admiralty, 16th July 1909, AIR 1/648, 17/122/398.

8.   *Flight*, No. 50, p. 790, 11th December 1909.

9.   *RUSI Journal*, Vol. LIV, May 1910, No. 387, p. 555 foll.

10.   AIR 1/648, 17/122/298.

11.   A copy of the pamphlet is to be found in AIR 1/648, 17/122/398.

12.   *NAS* pp. 14-18.

13.   *WIA*, Vol. I, pp. 158-9.

14.   WO paper 'Aviation in Foreign Countries', 15th November 1909, AIR 1/824, 204/5/69.

15.   WO paper 'Aeronautical Reports for 1910', undated, AIR 1/7, 6/77/3.

16.   The composition and functions of the Home Ports Defence Committee are described in a CID paper, 1st July 1909, AIR 1/2268, 209/70/224.

17.   Report of the Admiralty conference, 4th January 1910, AIR 1/654, 17/122/491.

18.   *WIA*, Vol. I, pp. 114-5, 156-7.

19.   *WIA*, Vol. I, pp. 171-4.

20.   *WIA*, Vol. I, p. 142.

21.   *WIA*, Vol. I, pp. 125-6.

22.   The recommendations of the Standing Sub-Committee on Aerial Navigation and the report of the Technical Sub-Committee are to be found in a CID paper dated 29th February 1912, AIR 1/21, 15/1/110.

23.   Report, 7th December 1912, AIR 1/657, 17/122/563.

24.   *WIA*, Vol. I, pp. 231-3.

25.   General Henderson, who was responsible for imposing this restriction on the size of engine produced, admitted in a note to the JWAC of 1st April 1916 that the policy had been mistaken. AIR 1/2319, 223/26.

26.   See Admiralty paper of 1913, 'Protection of British Dockyards from Aerial Attack', AIR 1/626, 17/42.

27.   *WIA*, Vol. III, pp. 74-76.

28.   Ibid.

29.   See Admiralty paper of 1913, 'Lecture on Aircraft for Naval Requirements', AIR 1/626, 17/47.

30.   See RN pamphlet, 'Lectures on Bomb-Sighting I-IV', 23rd April 1917, AIR 1/699, 27/3/404.

31. *Aeronautical Navigation* by Commander R.A. Newton R.N. 1909.

32. This was the Pattern 200 designed by Captain Creagh-Osborne R.N. in 1911.

33. A description of 'Sitwell's Drift Corrector' is to be found in AIR 1/349.

34. Sykes: *From Many Angles*, p. 94.

35. Huskinson: *Vision Ahead*, pp. 15-16.

36. AIR 1/769, 204/4/957.

37. The experiments carried out by the Admiralty from 1912 to 1914 are described by Group Captain R.H. Clark-Hall in a paper dated 24th November 1920, AIR 1/725, 118/1.

38. AIR 1/699, 17/122/781.

39. See Note 37.

40. See report on the Travers Bombsight, 20th December 1913, AIR 1/349.

41. Ibid.

42. AIR 1/762, 204/4/179.

43. AIR 1/757, 204/4/101.

44. Report, 9th May 1914, AIR 1/117, 15/40/27.

45. AIR 1/798, 204/4/1018.

46. AIR 1/810, 204/4/1225.

47. AIR 1/775, 204/4/368.

48. AIR 1/776, 204/4/388.

49. AIR 1/783, 204/4/517.

50. Sykes op. cit., p. 105.

Chapter 2

1. Sykes op. cit., pp. 111-12.

2. Sykes op. cit., p. 122.

3. Ibid.

4. Sykes op. cit. 123.

5. Boyle op. cit., pp. 115-123.

6. Memo. HQ RFC to HQ W/T Unit, 24th October 1914, AIR 1/834, 204/4/232.

7. Memo. by Major Musgrave 'Notes on Equipment for Bomb Dropping', 24th October 1914, AIR 1/834, 204/5/232.

8. *The Aeroplane*, 5th January 1916, p. 1.

9. *WIA*, Vol. III, p. 77.

10. See 'Airship Raids January-June 1915' — document produced by Intelligence Section, GHQ, Great Britain, revised ed. 1918, AIR 1/2319.

11. *WIA*, Vol. I, pp. 360-1.

12. *WIA*, Vol. I, pp. 371-2.

13. *WIA*, Vol. I, pp. 374-6.

14. *WIA*, Vol. I, p. 389.

15. *WIA*, Vol. I, pp. 389-90.

16. *WIA*, Vol. I, pp. 393-95.

17. *WIA*, Vol. I, pp. 395-401.

18. *WIA*, Vol. I, pp. 402-5.

19. AIR 1/2319, 223/29.

20. HQ RFC paper 'Bomb Drop-ping Attacks', 15th February 1915, AIR 1/921, 204/5/889.

21. *WIA*, Vol. II, pp. 95-6.

22. *WIA*, Vol. II, p. 105.

23. See Sir Ian Hamilton: *Gallipoli Diary*, London 1920, Vol. I, p. 8.

24. Paper by Wing Commander C.R. Samson, 2nd March 1915, AIR 1/672, 17/134/39.

25. AIR 1/672, 17/134/38.

26. *WIA*, Vol. II, p. 344.

27. *WIA*, Vol. II, pp. 349-53.

28. HQ RFC Memo. July 1915, AIR 1/921, 204/5/889.

29. Directive by the Chief of the General Staff, 24th July 1915, AIR 1/921, 204/5/889.

30. Boyle op. cit., pp. 29-30.

31. Boyle op. cit., pp. 92-95.

32. Boyle op. cit., pp. 96-9.

33. Boyle op. cit., pp. 100-101.

34. Boyle op. cit., p. 115.

35. Boyle op. cit., p. 121.

36. Boyle op. cit., p. 123.

37. Boyle op. cit., p. 125.

38. Ibid.

39. According to the Official His-tory, this posting was made at the request of the Admiralty (*WIA*, Vol. II, p. 57). Sykes too believed this to be the case (Sykes op. cit. 155). In fact, the Admiralty knew nothing of Sykes' appointment until it had been made, and were much

embarrassed by it. See minute DAS to First Sea Lord, 14th September 1915, AIR 1/361, 15/228/17.

40. Sykes op. cit., p. 165.

41. *WIA*, Vol. II, p. 124.

42. See paper by Group Captain R.H. Clark-Hall describing pre-war naval air experiments, 24th Novem-ber 1920, AIR 1/725, 118/1.

43. For descriptions of the 'nail' and 'lever' sights see air staff paper 'Short Notes on the Evolution and Theory of Bomb Sights', 8th Febru-ary 1921, AIR 1/674, 21/6/77.

44. Note by Musgrave, 26th De-cember 1914, AIR 1/834, 204/5/232.

45. Report, 2nd January 1915, AIR 1/826, 204/5/129.

46. For an account of how the CFS Sight was created (in spite of the indifference of the War Office) see the letter, dated 14th August 1920, which Bourdillon wrote to the Air Ministry seeking an award for his invention of the sight. AIR 1/22, 15/1/111. The Official History con-tains a very different account of Bourdillon's work. *WIA*, Vol. II, pp. 119-120.

47. Memo. by Major H.E. Wimperis, undated, but written in 1920 in connection with Bourdillon's claim for an award. AIR 1/22, 15/1/111.

48. For a description of the CFS sight and its method of operation see HMSO pamphlet 'Notes on Aerial Bombing Parts II and III', 1917, AIR 1/699, 27/3/415.

49.   Ronald   W.   Clark: *Tizard*, pp. 27-30.

50.   For a report on these experiments, 29th October 1915, see AIR 1/812, 204/4/1251.

51.   For the history of the development of French bombing plans, see the translation of a French official document 'History of the Evolution of the Plan of Bombardment by Aeroplanes', dated 18th November 1917, AIR 1/1976, 204/273/39.

52.   Ibid.

53.   Ibid.

54.   AIR 1/508, 16/3/52.

55.   Report by Captain W.L. Elder R.N. entitled 'No. 3 Wing R.N.A.S.' and dated 24th May 1917. AIR 1/2266, 209/70/18. Hereafter referred to as the Elder Report.

56.   Ibid.

57.   Report on the meeting at the Admiralty, 17th December 1915, AIR 1/625, 17/11.

Chapter 3

1.   Elder Report.

2.   See Admiralty paper 'Present Deficiencies and Future Requirements of the RNAS', 23rd March 1916, submitted by Rear-Admiral C.L. Vaughan-Lee, DAS, to the JWAC, AIR 1/2319, 223/26.

3.   Elder Report.

4.   Ibid.

5.   Ibid.

6.   Ibid.

7.   Policy statement on air bombing issued by GHQ, 3rd June 1916, AIR 1/978, 204/5/1139. Luxeuil was of course behind the French lines and some 200 miles from the area of British Army operations.

8.   Elder Report.

9.   AIR 1/633, 17/122/90.

10.   Ibid.

11.   Ibid.

12.   Ibid.

13.   *WIA*, Vol. II, p. 442.

14.   See undated post-war paper 'Design and Supply of Aircraft 1914-1918' by J.C. Nerney of the Air Historical Branch. AIR 1/678, 21/13/2186.

15.   Cecil Lewis: *Sagittarius Rising*, p. 64. For comments in a similar vein, see Huskinson: *Vision Ahead*, pp. 16-17.

16.   See, for example, letter Commodore RNAS Training Establishment, Cranwell to DAS Admiralty, 3rd May 1916, describing the bombing tests given to pilots before completing their courses. AIR 1/660, 17/122/631.

17.   Air Commodore Huskinson had completed about 14 hours solo when he was posted to France in April 1916. Huskinson op. cit, p. 16.

18.   There is a file dealing exclusive-

ly with cases of pilots being sent to France with inadequate training AIR 1/997, 204/5/1241.

19. *WIA*, Vol. III, pp. 268-9.

20. Memo. 'Duties of the RNAS and the RFC' by Major-General D. Henderson, 4th February 1916. AIR 1/270, 15/226/115.

21. Paper: 'Policy of Army Council with regard to Royal Flying Corps (Military Wing)' 2nd March 1916. AIR 1/270, 15/226/115. In reply to this charge, the Admiralty accused the War Office of trying to secure naval aircraft and equipment in order to conceal their own failure to plan for future military air requirements; and the official records provide much evidence to support this contention. It is therefore surprising to find Captain Roskill (*NAS*, p. XVII) accepting without question the accusations made by Sir David Henderson. It is worthy of note that charges of incompetence were at this time being levelled at the military air leaders from many quarters, and these led in the spring of 1916 to an investigation into the administration and command of the RFC by a committee under the chairmanship of Mr Justice Bailhache (*WIA*, Vol. III, pp. 274-5).

22. Minute First Sea Lord to DAS, 4th March 1916. AIR 1/270, 15/226/115.

23. 'Note by the Naval Representatives on the Joint War Air Committee', 23rd March 1916. It bore the names of Rear Admiral C.L. Vaughan-Lee, Commodore Murray F. Sueter and Squadron Commander W. Briggs. AIR 1/2319, 223/26.

24. Draft minute, 'Functions and Powers of the Committee', 29th March 1916. AIR 1/2319, 223/26.

25. 'Memorandum on the Principles Governing the Use of Aircraft in the Operations of War', 29th March 1916. AIR 1/2319, 223/26. It is probable that Admiral Sir Reginald Custance was the author (see *NAS*, pp. 336-7).

26. Remarks by the naval members on the draft minute 'Functions and powers of the Committee', 3rd April 1916. AIR 1/2319, 223/26.

27. *WIA*, Vol. III, pp. 269-70.

28. *WIA*, Vol. III, pp. 271-72.

29. *WIA*, Vol. III, pp. 272-74.

30. Captain Roskill castigates the Admiralty for not co-operating more fully with the Joint War Air Committee and the Air Board (*NAS*, pp. XVI-XVII). However, it would have been remarkable if the Admiralty had worked easily with these bodies whose main functions seem to have been to implement the policies already decided upon by the military air leaders.

31. Boyle op. cit., p. 204.

32. Minutes of a meeting with Colonel Barrés, held at the Admiralty, 22nd October 1916. AIR 1/515, 16/3/84(1).

33. Memo. Admiralty to the Air Board, 26th October 1916. AIR 1/515, 16/3/84(1).

34. Memo. Henderson to the Air Board, 31st October 1916. AIR 1/515, 16/3/84(1).

35. Memo. 29th October 1916, under Trenchard's signature, recorded a conversation between General Brancker and Trenchard concerning Colonel Barrés' proposals. AIR 1/515, 16/3/83(1).

36. Boyle op. cit., p. 204.

37. Letter Haig to W.O., 1st November 1916. AIR 2/123, file 'Sir Douglas Haig's criticism of Aerial Policy in France'.

38. The senior naval member of the Air Board.

39. Minutes of the 28th meeting of the Air Board, 1st November 1916. AIR 1/515, 16/3/84 (1).

40. Memo. Curzon to the War Committee, 9th November 1916. AIR 2/123, file 'Sir Douglas Haig's criticism of Aerial Policy in France'.

41. Ibid.

42. WIA, Vol. VI, p. 122.

43. Boyle op. cit., p. 205.

44. See note 39.

45. GHQ directive, 3rd June 1916. AIR 1/978, 204/5/1139.

46. Boyle op. cit., p. 204.

47. The CFS 'trombone' sight also allowed timing to be done on the actual target.

48. For details of the equal-distance sight see Admiralty pamphlet dated 1st July 1916. AIR 1/2103, 207/31.

49. The Isle of Grain experiments are described in an Admiralty booklet 'Lectures on Bomb-Sighting I-IV', 23rd April 1917. AIR 1/699, 23/3/404.

50. The report on the experiments at the Rossington Main Colliery was dated October 1916. AIR 2/133, 74018/16.

51. For a description of the CFS4B sight see 'Notes on Aerial Bombing Parts II and III', 1917. AIR 1/699, 27/3/415.

52. For descriptions of the Royal Aircraft Factory Periscope Bomb-sight Mk I (R.E.7) and Mk II (Martinsyde) see documents dated 5th August 1916. AIR 1/756, 204/4/91.

53. See 'Notes on Aerial Bombing Parts II and III', 1917 for a description of the CFS7. AIR 1/699, 27/3/415.

54. See air staff paper 'Short Notes on the Evolution of Theory of Bomb Sights', 8th February 1921. AIR 1/674, 21/6/77.

Chapter 4

1. Elder Report.

2. Ibid. See also Admiralty instructions to O.C. No. 3 Wing, 27th July 1916. AIR 1/115, 15/39/68.

3. Report of Aviation Conference held in London 4th July 1916. AIR 1/508, 16/3/52.

4. Letter Elder to the Admiralty,

22nd July 1916. AIR 1/113, 15/39/35.

5. Letter Elder to the Admiralty, 29th August 1916. AIR 1/113, 15/39/34.

6. Letter Elder to the Admiralty, 22nd October 1916. AIR 1/113, 15/39/35.

7. Elder Report.

8. Ibid.

9. Ibid.

10. *WIA*, Vol. III, pp. 280-1.

11. Admiralty instructions to O.C. No. 3 Wing, 27th July 1916. AIR 1/115, 15/39/68.

12. 'History of the Evolution of the Plan of Bombardment by Aeroplanes': translation of a French general staff document dated 18th November 1917. AIR 1/1976, 204/273/39.

13. File entitled 'Proposals for Bombing of Blast Furnaces in France, Belgium and Alsace-Lorraine', AIR 2/123.

14. Ibid.

15. Minutes of Air Board meeting of 11th December 1916. File as for Note 13.

16. Minute by Lord Sydenham, 14th December 1916. File as for Note 13.

17. For details of this aircraft see K. Munson: *Bombers 1914-19*, pp. 134-136.

18. See Munson: *Bombers 1914-19*, pp. 98-99.

19. Wing Commander R.B. Davies, V.C. D.S.O. was awarded his Victoria Cross while serving with the RNAS in Gallipoli. *WIA*, Vol. II, p. 67. He continued to serve in the Navy after the war and reached the rank of vice-admiral. Shortly before his death in 1966, he completed his memoirs entitled *Sailor in the Air*.

20. Report on Breguet aircraft by Wing Commander R.B. Davies, 4th September 1916. AIR 1/115, 15/39/51.

21. Report by Captain Elder to the Air Board and recorded in the form of a minute by Captain R.M. Groves R.N., assistant secretary to the Air Board, 25th October 1916. AIR 2/123, file entitled 'Report on Raid by British and French Airmen on Oberndorf'.

22. AIR 1/114, 15/39/46.

23. See note 21.

24. Lord Tiverton later became the 2nd Earl of Halsbury. A brief outline of his career in the RNAS is contained in a memo written by Lord Tiverton to the head of his directorate at the Air Ministry, 2nd July 1918. Halsbury Papers.

25. Memo. written by Lord Tiverton, April 1916 while serving in the Air Department. Halsbury papers.

26. Davies: *Sailor in the Air*, p. 147.

27. Ibid.

28. Report on the Oberndorf raid, No. 3 Wing to the Admiralty, 12th October 1916. AIR 1/111, 15/39/1. Pilots' reports on this raid are con-

P

tained in AIR 1/114, 15/39/46.

29. Davies op. cit. p. 151.

30. The extract from the *Frankfurter Zeitung* is contained in a paper 'Daily Aeronautical Report', dated 31st October 1916. File as for note 21.

31. Minute Captain R.M. Groves R.N. to members of the Air Board, 2nd November 1916. File as for note 21.

32. Concerning formation flying with Sopwiths and Breguets see AIR 1/662, 17/122/668.

33. Davies op. cit., p. 151.

34. Report 3 Wing to the Admiralty, 23rd October 1916. AIR 1/111, 15/39/1.

35. Davies op. cit., p. 154.

36. Davies op. cit., p. 155.

37. *WIA*, Vol. VI, pp. 118-120.

38. Minute Captain R.M. Groves to members of the Air Board, 25th October 1916. File as for note 21.

39. *WIA*, Vol. VI, p. 120.

40. 'Remarks on Experience Gained in Air Raids and on Probable Requirements as to Types of Machines in the Future', by Wing Commander R.B. Davies, 4th January 1917. AIR 1/113, 15/39/35.

41. Memo. Elder to the Admiralty, December 1916. AIR 1/113, 15/39/35.

42. Elder Report.

43. *WIA*, Vol. VI, p. 120.

44. Ibid.

45. See Munson: *Bombers 1914-1919*, pp. 150-2.

46. *WIA*, Vol. VI, pp. 120-1.

47. Report O.C. Handley Page Squadron to O.C. No. 3 Wing, 17th March 1917. AIR 1/113, 15/39/35.

48. *WIA*, Vol. VI, p. 121.

49. Elder Report.

50. *WIA*, Vol. VI, p. 121.

51. *WIA*, Vol. VI, p. 122.

52. *WIA*, Vol. IV, p. 81-2.

53. For details of this report see *WIA*, Vol. VI, pp. 167-8.

54. Ibid.

55. See Munson: *Bombers 1914-19*, pp. 137-9.

56. Report by Captain C.L. Lambe, 3rd February 1918. AIR 1/35, 15/1/216. See also *WIA*, Vol. IV, pp.106-8.

57. *WIA*, Vol. III, Ch. VI. See Groves: 'Behind the Smoke Screen', pp. 128-133.

58. *WIA*, Vol. III, p. 353.

59. For an account of the Zeppelin raids up to the end of 1916 see *WIA*, Vol. III, Chs. II and III.

60. *WIA*, Vol. III, pp. 243-8.

61. For examples of navigational difficulties experienced by Zeppelin commanders see *WIA*, Vol. III, pp. 109-112 and pp. 135-140.

Chapter 5

1. *WIA*, Vol. V, p. 18.

2. *WIA*, Vol. V, pp. 19-20.

3. *WIA*, Vol. V, p. 20.

4. *WIA*, Vol. V, pp. 20-22.

5. *WIA*, Vol. V, pp. 25-28.

6. *WIA*, Vol. V, p. 29.

7. This was in fact the object of the offensive Haig was planning.

8. *WIA*, Vol. V, pp. 29-31.

9. *WIA*, Vol. V, pp. 31-32.

10. *WIA*, Vol. V, pp. 36-38.

11. *Flying*, Vol. I, No. 25, 11th July 1917, p. 462.

12. *Flying*, Vol. I, No. 26, 18th July 1917, p. 479.

13. *WIA*, Vol. V, pp. 38-39.

14. For this report see *WIA*, Appendix Vol. Appendix II.

15. *WIA*, Vol. VI, p. 10.

16. *WIA*, Vol. VI, p. 6.

17. Letter Haig to CIGS, 15th September 1917. *WIA*, Appendix Vol., Appendix III.

18. Boyle op. cit., p. 236.

19. Memo. by Sir David Henderson, 19th July 1917. *WIA*, Appendix Vol., Appendix I.

20. Boyle op. cit., pp. 232-3

21. *WIA*, Vol. VI, p.13.

22. *WIA*, Vol. VI, pp. 19-22.

23. *WIA*, Vol. VI, pp. 22-23.

24. *WIA*, Vol. VI, p. 26.

25. *WIA*, Vol. VI, pp. 26-27.

26. Sykes op.cit., pp. 226-7.

27. Report by Lord Tiverton, submitted to the Air Board on 3rd September 1917. AIR 1/462, 15/312/121.

28. After the war, Trenchard told H.A. Jones that the French had put every difficulty in his way. See AIR 8/167, file entitled 'Private interview with Lord Trenchard. Dictated notes by H.A. Jones 11th April 1934'.

29. Statement by Trenchard at a meeting of the Air Policy Committee, 28th November 1917. AIR 1/678, 21/13/2102.

30. For an account of the mutinies see Major-General Sir Edward Spears: *Two Men who Saved France*, Eyre and Spottiswoode, 1966, p. 21 foll., pp. 97-8.

31. Correspondence Pétain-Haig, Sept-Oct. 1917, AIR 1/678, 21/13/2102.

32. Minutes of the meeting of the Air Policy Committee held on 28th November 1917. AIR 1/678, 21/13/2102.

33. *WIA*, Vol. VI, p. 123.

34. *WIA*, Vol. VI, pp. 124-5.

35. *WIA*, Vol. VI, p. 18.

36. Letter Tiverton to Kerr, 8th October 1917. Halsbury papers.

37. Memo. by Admiral Kerr, 11th November 1917. AIR 1/678,

21/13/2102; Kerr: *Land Sea and Air*, pp. 289-91.

38. See AIR 8/167, file entitled 'Private Interview with Lord Trenchard. Dictated notes by H.A. Jones, 11th April 1934'.

39. *WIA*, Vol. VI, p. 19.

40. *WIA*, Vol. VI, p. 21.

41. Letter Kerr to Tiverton, 22nd November 1917. Halsbury papers.

42. Letter Kerr to Tiverton, 30th November 1917. Halsbury papers.

43. Bombing Report, 2nd November 1917. Halsbury Papers.

44. Paper by Wing Commander C.R.J. Randall, 12th November 1917. AIR 1/460, 15/312/97.

45. Memo. January 1918. AIR 1/463, 15/312/137.

46. Paper entitled 'Long Distance Bombing', 26th November 1917. AIR 1/725, 97/7.

47. Report Lambe to Vice-Admiral, Dover Patrol, 31st October 1917. AIR 1/640. 'Report by Captain Lambe after Visit to 'A' Naval Squadron at Ochey'.

48. A complete list of the industrial targets bombed by the squadrons of the 41st Wing and the Independent Force, October 1917 to November 1918, is to be found in *WIA*, Appendix Vol., Appendix XIII. A narrative of the operations is to be found in the *WIA*, Vol. VI, Ch. IV.

49. A pamphlet describing these sights is to be found in AIR 1/699, 27/3/435.

50. A total of 19,750 of these sights was produced during the years 1917 and 1918. See air staff paper, 8th February 1921, 'Short Notes on the Evolution and Theory of Bomb Sights', Appendix I. AIR 1/674, 21/6/77.

51. For a description of the nevative lens sight, see H.M.S.O. pamphlet (1917) 'Notes on Aerial Bombing Parts II and III'. AIR 1/699, 27/3/415.

52. The Course Setting Bombsight Mk I is described in an Admiralty pamphlet of January 1918. AIR 1/2103, 207/30/34.

53. For a review of RFC pilot and observer training see *WIA*, Vol. III, pp. 292-301 and Vol. V, Ch. VIII.

54. *WIA*, Vol. V, p. 469 footnote. This figure had increased to 48½ hours by September 1917.

55. *WIA*, Vol. V, pp. 438-443. Also undated paper 'Summary of Notes on Training of RNAS Personnel'. AIR 1/678, 21/13/2082.

56. Details of the establishment of this course, in October 1917, are given in AIR 1/30. 15/1/151.

57. The correspondence relating to the establishment of this school is contained in AIR 1/122, 15/40/136.

Chapter 6

1. Boyle op. cit., p. 219.

2. Boyle op. cit., p. 208.

3. Sykes op. cit., pp 176-7, p. 224.

4. Memo. Pink to DCAS, 17th April 1918. AIR 1/460, 15/312/101.

5. The papers concerning the Strategic Council are contained in AIR 1/450, 15/312/4.

6. Minute CTD to the secretary of the Strategic Council, 22nd April 1918. AIR 1/463, 15/312/137.

7. Paper dated 24th April 1918. AIR 1/450, 5/312/4.

8. *WIA*, Vol. VI, p. 28 foll.

9. *WIA*, Vol. VI, pp. 37-8.

10. *WIA*, Vol. VI, pp. 45-51.

11. *WIA*, Vol. VI, pp. 31-2.

12. *WIA*, Vol. VI, p. 166.

13. *WIA*, Vol. VI, p. 169.

14. Report entitled 'Long Distance Bombing', 26th November 1917. AIR 1/725, 97/7.

15. *WIA*, Vol. VI, p. 169.

16. Sykes op. cit. p. 228.

17. *WIA*, Vol. VI, pp. 101-117.

18. Memo Weir to War Cabinet, 23rd May 1918. *WIA*, Appendix Vol., Appendix VII.

19. Tiverton to CAS, 22nd May 1918. AIR 1/460, 15/312/101.

20. Paper May 1918. AIR 1/460, 15/312/101.

21. Paper June 1918. AIR 1/460, 15/312/97.

22. Paper July 1918. AIR 1/460, 15/312/97.

23. Paper 27th May 1918. AIR 1/460, 15/312/101.

24. AIR 1/460, 15/312/101.

25. Memo. Tiverton to DFO, 10th June 1918, AIR 1/460, 15/312/97.

26. See AIR 2/76, file entitled 'Formation of Independent Force in England'.

27. *WIA*, Vol. VI, p. 173-4.

28. Paper by Lord Tiverton, 17th August 1918. AIR 1/460, 15/312/97.

29. Memo. Tiverton to DFO, August 1918. Halsbury Papers.

30. Memo. DFO to CAS, September 1918. AIR 1/460, 15/312/101. See also Groves op. cit., pp. 137-8.

31. M.M. Patrick: *The United States in the Air*, 1928, quoted by Groves op. cit., pp. 136-7. See also Sykes op. cit., p. 146 and 231.

32. Paper by Lord Tiverton: 'The Possibilities of Long Distance Bombing from the Present Day until September 1919', 1st October 1918. AIR 1/460, 15/312/101.

33. Paper by Lord Tiverton, 11th November 1918. AIR 1/460, 15/312/101.

34. The operations of the bomber force are described in *WIA*, Vol. VI, Ch. IV.

35. *WIA*, Vol. VI, p. 132.

36. *WIA*, Vol. VI, p. 142.

37. *WIA*, Vol. VI, pp. 145-6.

38. *WIA*, Vol. VI, pp. 147-8

39. AIR 1/2104 207/36.

40. The official German view concerning the effects of the air raids was identical to the findings of the British Commission. See a paper by Major Grosskreutz in *Die Luftwacht*, October 1928. A translation of this paper is to be found in AIR 1/711, 27/13/2214.

41. *WIA*, Vol. VI, p. 154.

42. *WIA*, Vol. VI, p. 130.

43. Report of the British Commission, January 1920, p. 36. AIR 1/2104, 207/36.

44. *WIA*, Vol. VI, pp. 153-4.

45. These statistics were given to the Air Ministry by the Air Historical Branch in a letter dated 11th December 1923. AIR 9/69 Folio 21.

46. Much of this material is derived from two reports compiled by officers of No. 7 Training Group, RAF, after staff visits to the Independent Force and No. 5 Group. The first report, dated 9th September 1918, was written by Brigadier-General F.V. Holt, the second, dated 11th October 1918, by Lieutenant-Colonel J.T. Babington and Captain G.E. Godsave. AIR 1/454, 15/312/27.

47. For this correspondence see AIR 1/460, 15/312/100.

48. For the Orfordness report on Cloud Flying, dated 21st December 1917, see AIR 1/463, 15/312/137.

49. *WIA*, Vol. VI, p. 133.

Reflections of the Air War

1. *WIA*, Vol. VI, p. 552.

2. For an important account of the development of strategic policy in the RAF during the inter-war years see Webster and Frankland op. cit., Ch. II.

3. The great value of operational research in the Second World War is shown in Part II of *Studies of War* by P.M.S. Blackett, Oliver and Boyd, 1962.

4. *WIA*, Vol. V, p. 471.

Bibliography

Ashmore, Major-General, E.B., *Air Defence*. Longmans, Green, 1929.

Beaverbrook, Lord, *Men and Power*. Hutchinson, 1956.

Boyle, Andrew, *Trenchard*. Collins, 1962.

Clark, Ronald, W., *Tizard*. Methuen, 1965.

Davies, Vice-Admiral Richard Bell, *Sailor in the Air*. Peter Davies, 1967.

Douglas of Kirtleside, Marshal of the Royal Air Force Lord, *Years of Combat*. Collins, 1963.

Fredette, Major Raymond H., *The First Battle of Britain 1917-1918*. Cassell, 1966.

Grey, G.C., *A History of The Air Ministry*. Allen and Unwin, 1940.

Groves, Brigadier-General P.R.C., *Behind the Smoke Screen*. Faber and Faber, 1934.

Hughes, Arthur J., *History of Air Navigation*. Allen and Unwin, 1946.

Huskinson, Air Commodore P., *Vision Ahead*. Werner Laurie, 1949.

Joubert de la Ferté, Air Chief Marshal Sir Philip, *The Third Service*. Thames and Hudson, 1955.

Kerr, Admiral Mark, *Land, Sea and Air*. Longmans, Green, 1927.

Lanchester, F.W., *Aircraft in Warfare*. Constable, 1916.

Lewis, Cecil, *Sagittarius Rising*. Peter Davies, 1936.

Lewis, Cecil, *Farewell to Wings*. Temple Press, 1964.

MacDonagh, Michael, *In London During the Great War*. Eyre and Spottiswoode, 1935.

Morison, Frank, *War on Great Cities*. Faber and Faber, 1937.

Moyes, Philip J.R., *Bomber Squadrons of the RAF and their Aircraft*. Macdonald, 1964.

Munson, Kenneth, *Bombers 1914-1919*. Blandford Press, 1968.

Raleigh, Sir Walter and Jones, H.A., *The War in the Air*, 6 volumes and 1 volume of appendices. Oxford University Press, 1922-37.

Saundby, Air Marshal Sir Robert, *Air Bombardment*. Chatto and Windus, 1961.

Saunders, Hilary St. George, *Per Ardua. The Rise of British Air Power 1911-39*. Oxford University Press, 1944.

Slessor, Wing Commander J.C., *Air Power and Armies*. Oxford University Press, 1936.

Slessor, Marshal of the Royal Air Force Sir John, *The Central Blue*. Cassell, 1956.

Strange, Lieutenant-Colonel L.A., *Recollections of an Airman*. John Hamilton, 1933.

Sykes, Major-General Sir Frederick, *From Many Angles*. Harrap, 1942.

Webster, Sir Charles and Frankland, Noble, *The Strategic Air Offensive against Germany 1939-1945*. H.M.S.O. 1961 Volume I.

Index

Falkenburg, 164
'Flaming Onions' (German night-flying aid) 201
'Flight', 28
Flock Bombing, 200
'Flying', 133
Foch, General (later Marshal), 178, 195
Folkstone, 131
France, 34, 55, 67, 68, 69, 92, 123, 134, 137, 147, 176, 178, 206, 212
Frankfurt, 147, 155, 193, 194
'Frankfurter Zeitung', 114-5
Freiburg, 118, 123, 165
French Air Service, 65, 76-8, 113, 115-6, 191, 212
Friedrichshafen, 58

Gallipoli, 69
German Air Service, 128, 210-11
Germany, 18, 19, 20, 21, 25, 28, 30, 31, 32, 33, 34, 39, 40, 41, 118, 123, 127, 132-3, 138, 150, 187, 188, 203, 206, 209, 211, 212
Ghent, 56, 127
Gloucester Castle (Hospital ship), 123
Gontrode, 130
Grain, Isle of, 99
Grey, C.G., 53-4
Grey, Squadron Commander S.D.A., 63
Groves, Brig.-Gen. P.R.C., 175, 189
Groves, Wing Captain R.M., 115

Hagen, 187
Hagendingen, 116, 122, 196
Hague Conference, 25

Haig, Field-Marshal Sir Douglas, 17, 18, 22-3, 48-9, 68, 80, 81, 91, 93-4, 95, 96, 97-8, 132, 134, 139, 140, 141, 148, 149, 150, 206
Hamburg, 48, 186
Handley Page Company, 77
Henderson, Lt.-Gen. Sir David, 16, 23, 36, 50, 51, 68, 69, 84-5, 90-1, 92, 95, 96, 97, 109, 139-40, 141, 142, 204, 205, 206
Höchst, 156
Hoeppner, General von, 130
Holland, 31, 79
Huskinson, Air Commodore P., 44

Independent Force (R.A.F.), 18, 127, 142, 178, 183, 184, 186, 188, 189, 190, 193, 194, 195, 198, 199, 212
Industries, Enemy War, aero-engines, 157, 182, chemicals, 108, 155, 156, 181, 182, 188, 190, 191, explosives, 108, 157, iron and steel, 108, 109, 115-6, 144, 150, 157, 181-2, 187, 190, 191, magnetos, 157, 182, munitions, 108

Jackson, Admiral Sir Henry, 86
Joint War Air Committee, 85, 86, 87, 88, 89, 90, 140
Jones, H.A. (Official Historian), 22, 206
Juniville, 191

Kaiserslautern, 195
Karlsruhe, 165